SMOKY MOUNTAIN COUNTRY
MINNESOTA
WISCONSIN
IOWA
ILLINOIS
INDIANA
OHIO
NEW YORK
MAINE
VERMONT
NEW HAMPSHIRE
MASSACHUSETTS
CONN.
PENNSYLVANIA
N.J.
MARYLAND
WEST VIRGINIA
VIRGINIA
OHIO RIVER
KENTUCKY
TENNESSEE
CAROLINA
SOUTH CAROLINA
GEORGIA
ALABAMA
MISSISSIPPI
ARKANSAS

Smoky Mountain Country

AMERICAN FOLKWAYS

EDITED BY ERSKINE CALDWELL

EDITED BY ERSKINE CALDWELL

SMOKY MOUNTAIN COUNTRY

BY NORTH CALLAHAN

DUELL, SLOAN & PEARCE · NEW YORK
LITTLE, BROWN & COMPANY · BOSTON

DUELL, SLOAN AND PEARCE—LITTLE, BROWN
BOOKS ARE PUBLISHED BY
LITTLE, BROWN AND COMPANY
IN ASSOCIATION WITH
DUELL, SLOAN & PEARCE, INC.

*Published simultaneously
in Canada by McClelland and Stewart Limited*

PRINTED IN THE UNITED STATES OF AMERICA

To

My Father and Mother
True Offspring of the Smokies

Foreword

Who knows thee well is sure to love,
Where'er his wandering footsteps rove.
And backward ever turn to thee
With fond, regretful memory,
Feeling his heart impatient burn
Among thy mountains to return.

THIS anonymous poem expresses well the feelings of a displaced Smoky Mountaineer who has gone far from his native region — but who returns every chance he gets. Among my reasons for writing this book must be listed a warm attachment to the mountain country of Tennessee and North Carolina, and if this regard is tempered with a recognition of all the faults of that storied land, the feeling nevertheless remains.

On the day I was born, along about suppertime, my mother could look out from the pillow which crowned her best featherbed and see the blue forms of the Smokies, hazy and lovely on the near horizon. This natural tableau set against the clear East Tennessee sky has been my favorite scene from the time I opened my eyes. Though apt description was long denied me, it made little difference, for the Smokies can never exactly be described anyway. In the other part of the picturesque frame building, my father went about his daily work as owner and operator of a country store. Its location, to be precise, was at Fork Creek in Monroe County, about halfway between the towns of Sweetwater and Madisonville.

My first memories of the store are of country musicians whanging on banjos and sawing on fiddles around the stove while they helped themselves to generous portions of crackers from the barrel and cheese from the hoop. The tunes they played are heard today, only more so, for they have been transferred to a million jukeboxes. A vivid parenthesis in my early existence was that occasioned by the eating of a half-plug of Apple Tobacco, simply because I thought that the popular expression, "eatin' terbaccer," meant just that. The deadly misery which overtook me behind the counter as a result, and the throwing up of everything including what seemed to be the bottom of my stomach, helped to keep this clandestine episode clear in my memory as time went on.

School was an itinerant thing, my family moving many times, but always staying at least within sight of the mountains. My parents loved these mountains, and my mother would sometimes sit and look at them for a long time without saying a word. Perhaps my father expressed it when he quoted from the Bible: *I will lift up mine eyes unto the hills, from whence cometh my help.* Living for a time at beauteous Montvale, where the Smokies form an especially pictorial backdrop, we went to church at Carpenter's Camp Ground and heard about the Great Revival of 1800, from which such churches got their names. Our language was typical of the mountains, and it was years before I understood why our invalid cousin, who read a lot in bed, named two of his sons Milton and Shakespere.

The years that followed were filled with the great heights

and depths of boyhood. Across the dimming panorama of yesteryear flit still-warm memories — walking miles to one-room schools and carrying lunch in a lard bucket; eating cornbread baked on the hearth in an iron baker; waiting beside the chicken house for the hens to lay eggs so I could hurry with one to the nearby grocery store, there to buy an "egg's worth of chocolate bears"; listening to Grandpa tell how *his* grandpa "fit" in the battle of King's Mountain; avidly reading books when I was supposed to be herding cows in the meadow; wondering why one of my grand-fathers was on the Union side of the Civil War between the States, while the other was a Confederate; reading again and again the framed motto in our parlor: *I slept and dreamed that life was beauty; I woke and found that life was duty;* hoeing corn in summer, chopping firewood in winter, swim-ming in creeks beside the railroad tracks and occasionally throwing a rock at the passing trains; making frequent trips into the mountains and being awed by their big, silent peaks; having Christmas in the country and getting off the Yule tree a stick of striped candy, an orange, and a penny pencil — and once, thrillingly, a "Franch harp"; smelling the rich aroma of Arbuckle's coffee just as the sun arose to catch the dew on the grass; calling doodlebugs out of their holes; ad-miring the uniform of an uncle who came back from World War I and rode majestically up to our house in a brand-new Model T. It seems that we lived in and near Indian towns, judging from their names: Sweetwater, Niota, Etowah, Tel-lico Plains, and then Chattanooga. Now and then my two brothers, two sisters, and I picked up arrowheads said to have been shot by the Cherokees, among whom was supposed to be an ancestor of ours.

Following a stint at universities in Chattanooga and Knox-

ville, and later at Columbia and New York University, I
entered teaching, but my course soon turned journalistic.
After working for newspapers in Tennessee, I followed the
early lead of David Crockett and Sam Houston and veered
into Texas. More years on newspapers and hearing tall tales
of the Lone Star State made me wonder if, by comparison,
any state such as Tennessee or North Carolina could amount
to anything at all. Next came my turn among the towers of
Manhattan, which seemed as high as some of the Smokies
but less inviting. In fact, the longer I live in New York
City, the better I like the Great Smoky Mountains. Despite
this natural carping at the wonderful metropolis, a column
for newspapers about the big city sets forth my regular reactions to it, among them many that are good. But every
chance I get, using any excuse I can manufacture, I run back
to the country of my earlier days and live again among the
God-made skyscrapers where the streets are winding trails
and the avenues are covered with laurel and rhododendron.

Acknowledgments

Besides first-hand knowledge, personal interviews, and letters, I have made extensive use of newspaper and magazine
files in writing this book. On some phases of the subject matter, many volumes have been published; on others, none at
all. Among the books I read were *History of the Lost State
of Franklin,* by S. C. Williams; *Old Frontiers,* by J. P. Brown;
The Raven: A Biography of Sam Houston, by Marquis
James; *Tennessee: A Guide to the Volunteer State,* by the
Federal Writers' Project; *The Tennessee,* by Donald David-
son; *Democracy on the March,* by David Lilienthal; *The Oak*

Ridge Story, by G. O. Robinson, Jr.; *Land of High Horizons,*
by Elizabeth S. Bowman; *The Great Smoky Mountains,* by
Laura Thornburgh; *Our Southern Highlanders,* by Horace
Kephart; *The Great Smokies and the Blue Ridge,* by Rod-
erick Peattie; *Bob Taylor and the Agrarian Revolt in Tennessee,* by Daniel M. Robison; *Tennessee: A History,* by
Philip M. Hamer; *From Frontier to Plantation in Tennessee,*
by T. P. Abernethy; *The Age of Hate,* by George Fort Milton; *Civil War and Reconstruction,* by J. G. Randall; *The
Coming of the Civil War,* by Avery Craven; *History of Popular Music in America,* by Sigmund Spaeth; *White Spirituals
in the Southern Uplands,* by G. P. Jackson; *Songs of the Old
Campground,* by L. L. McDowell; *American Mountain Songs,*
by E. P. Richardson; *Songs Sung in the Southern Appalachians,* by M. E. Henry; *Exploring the South,* by Vance, Ivey,
and Bond; and *Southern Politics,* by V. O. Key, Jr.

I wish to express my appreciation to the staffs of the New
York Public Library, the Chattanooga Public Library, the
Lawson-McGhee Library in Knoxville, the Library of Con-
gress, Columbia University Library, New York University
Library, the Cleveland (Tennessee) Library, Crestwood
(New York) Library, the Tennessee Historical Society, the
East Tennessee Historical Society, the university libraries of
Tennessee, Chattanooga, and North Carolina, as well as to
those of various other libraries and collections in Tennessee,
North Carolina, Georgia, Virginia, and Kentucky.

Individuals who have been extremely helpful include Dr.
David A. Lockmiller, Dr. E. S. Lindsey, and Gilbert Govan
of the University of Chattanooga; Senator Estes Kefauver and
his staff; Governor Gordon Browning of Tennessee and his
staff; Tennessee State Librarian Dan M. Robison; John
Oliver, W. L. Sturdevant, Maurice Henle, B. L. Foy, and the

information staff of the Tennessee Valley Authority; Colonel Milton Ochs and Alfred Mynders of the Chattanooga *Times;* the information staff of Oak Ridge; Dr. William E. Cole, Miss Bertie Wenning, Eugene E. Patton, Carl Jones, Carroll E. Mealey, Jr.; Clyde B. Emert, Miss Ruth Chambers, William R. McDaniel, Robert L. Taylor, Miss Adelaide Rowell; Milton, Shakespere, Gertrude, Agnes, Gladys, Raymond, Robert, and Jesse Callahan; John, James, and Walter North; Miss Gertrude Richesin, Mrs. Walter Riddle, Miss Anna B. Miller, Mrs. Rachel Miller, Mr. and Mrs. John M. Connor; William Postlewaite, Fred S. Lloyd, Clarence Griffin, B. Arp Lowrance, Don McKay, G. R. Molesworth, Ray B. Slagle, John C. Pemberton, Lowell W. Brown; Ed Smith of the Knoxville *News-Sentinel;* Walter Michael, Edward J. Meeman, Robert H. White, B. T. Gregory, J. Will Foster, Carl Haverlin, Mrs. C. M. Waugh, William T. Latham, J. Pope Dyer; and, particularly, my wife.

NORTH CALLAHAN

Crestwood, New York

Contents

CONTENTS

Smoky Mountain Country

I

Birthplace of a State

For many restless men of the western part of North Carolina there was, in the latter part of the eighteenth century, a strong pull farther westward. This magnetic attraction led over that part of the Appalachians known as the Great Smoky Mountains, northwestward to their upper reaches. Some of these men went seeking fortunes, some to escape debtors, others just went. They pushed their lithe ponies through the high passes or drove their oxcarts through precipitous trails, seeking the greener fields which they had pursued all the way from Scotland and northern Ireland to Pennsylvania and down to the Caroline. The more substantial pioneers, once they had viewed this well-favored land, stayed, and for the most part so did their offspring. The descendants generally have felt that the Smoky Mountain Country, which extends from the Kentucky and Virginia state lines southward through East Tennessee and western North Carolina to Georgia, is as near the Promised Land as they could wish for on this earth.

Groups in search of land quickly staked out claims to it, feeling that legal details could be worked out later. Others had little desire to acquire real property, never having had any, so became perpetual squatters in the wake of the pioneer vanguard, never taking root, always shifting and sometimes away from the law.

Solid individuals, however, soon emerged as leaders. In 1768, almost a year before Daniel Boone came out of Kentucky to view from the Cumberland Gap the beauties of what is now upper East Tennessee, a man named William Bean had dared to clear the land in the Valley of Watauga and build his cabin there. The next year he went back to Virginia and brought his family to their new home in the wilderness. Soon some of his kinfolks and neighbors joined them.

In the fore of the first westward group from North Carolina was James Robertson, a sturdy Scots-Irishman whom Daniel Boone had told about the new "land of milk and honey." After he had viewed from an adjoining mountain the verdant grandeur of the Watauga Valley, Robertson made haste to return to North Carolina and bring his own family there. But his excitement and eagerness were greater than his sense of direction. He was no Daniel Boone. On the way back, Robertson got lost in the wild, unexplored mountains and wandered for days in a great circle. The steep terrain became so difficult that he had to turn his horse loose and proceed on foot. Finally, in anguish at not knowing where he was, he fell physically exhausted on the side of a rugged peak. He was freezing and his last food was gone. In desperation, he prayed as he collapsed. His prayer was answered. In a little while, some passing hunters stumbled over his unconscious form, and he was saved.

Soon afterward, Robertson led a group of his followers from North Carolina to Watauga. William Bean greeted them with these words: "I desire you to make my home your home. From this moment, as long as it is convenient to you, you are members of my family." Such sentiments characterized the hospitality that was to become generally representative of the people of the Smoky Mountain Country. James Robertson soon became one of the pillars of the new colony. Later he was to push even farther westward and earn the name of the father of the state called Tennessee.

The Watauga settlement was the signal for others to follow rapidly. John Carter and Joseph Parker established a trading post on the Holston River near the junction of its forks. Eastward along the same river, two brothers, Evan and John Shelby, moved in, while about the same time Jacob Brown posted a claim in the Nolichucky Valley.

Living in Virginia was a prosperous young storekeeper named John Sevier. He heard of the new country below the Blue Ridge to which so many of the folks of Virginia and North Carolina were moving. Their enthusiasm was enough to make up his mind, and in 1772 he closed his business and moved his family to Watauga. Sevier was to become the greatest Indian fighter of his day, and play a vital part in the growth of a new region and the founding of a state. He was to free East Tennessee from the grip of the savage and to emerge as its foremost leader, whose role, according to Theodore Roosevelt, was "much greater than that of George Rogers Clark, although the latter had more men with which to operate." Yet Sevier has been largely neglected by historians.

These leaders were typical of the best settlers of the uplands of Tennessee and North Carolina. Here the frontiersmen found what they had long been seeking: home and freedom. The wildness of the new land appealed to the daring in their natures. They did not shrink from a fight, either with Indians or with others. Men like Sevier were admired because they were natural-born leaders who could take their followers to victory. In return, they had the undying, almost fanatical loyalty of men who placed such devotion above all other sentiments. The relationship was like that which their forefathers cherished in the Scottish highlands where the clansmen instinctively followed the call of their chieftains. Nowhere in the world did the extension of family loyalty to the community leader exceed that of this early frontier.

The settlements stemming from the Watauga and along the Holston River did not take long to grow. Soon wagon roads were built which led to North Carolina as well as Virginia. Many settlers came into Tennessee by the Good Spur route, which extended from western Virginia down into the Holston valleys. Others came across the Stone, Yellow, and Bald Mountains of the Allegheny range, which stretched above the Great Smokies along the Carolina border into southern Virginia. Contrary to some historical accounts, because of the comparatively easy accessibility of these routes it was not hard for the earliest white pioneers from those two states to move into upper East Tennessee. The Holston and Watauga people also helped the migration by the close contact which they maintained with old friends and relatives in their home states, and the farms of the early Tennesseans soon were well-forged links in a chain extending back across the state borders.

The government established by the Watauga settlers was to stand as a model. It was the first free and independent government in America. One must remember that, at this time, the Thirteen Colonies were still under the rule of the British, a rule which these early Tennesseans were to do much to remove. In May 1772 the form of the Watauga government was put into writing. It provided for five commissioners, a majority of whom were to decide all matters of controversy, and whose principal duty was to govern the people for their common welfare. The first five commissioners were John Sevier, James Robertson, Charles Roberson, Zachariah Isbell, and John Carter. Their descendants live in this same region today.

At first, the Watauga Association recognized no higher power except God. It was a government entered into by the free will of every individual. The commission performed all major legal functions, including arraignment, trial, conviction, and execution of such offenders as horsethieves; and all these steps could be taken — and were — within an hour. No drawn-out appeals in this judicial body. Promptness was their credo — and besides, there was no jail.

A suspicious character was spotted almost as soon as he arrived in this settlement where everyone knew everybody else. If the stranger gave his name as John Eveningstar or Henry Moonglow or Richard Weatherstone, it was more than likely that he would shortly be waited upon by a committee, who, after a proper interval of at least several minutes of questioning, would politely inform him that they could not find his name in the Book of Genesis, and therefore concluded that he was living under an assumed one. What was more, in their estimation, he had probably stolen a horse, and had better move on before nightfall to some other neck of the woods — which invariably he did.

John Sevier presided over the first of these courts. A typical case that came before it is revealing. Two men were charged with stealing horses. After a brief trial, they received their sentence:

> It is ordered that they be confined in the publick pillory for the space of an hour, and that each of them have both of their ears nailed to the pillory and severed from their heads. That they receive at the publick whipping post, 39 lashes upon their bare backs, well laid on, and that each of them be branded upon their right cheek with the letter T, and that this sentence be put into effect between the hours of 12 and 4 this afternoon.

Asked if this were not a hard sentence, Sevier replied: "What would you say if your horse had been stolen? Think what our horses mean to us, they pack furs, carry us along the trail, they draw the plow, they drag from the forests the logs from which we make our cabins. These men stole horses. Worse still, they are setting a bad example to the Cherokees who are learning to steal the faithful animals. . . . Death would be a mild penalty for a horse thief. So you see, our verdict is merciful."

It is not strange that Sevier immediately became a leader of the settlements. He was a strikingly handsome man, slightly under six feet tall, lean and muscular, and quick in movement. His face was of classical mold and his hair a rich, curly blond. He usually dressed in a buckskin hunting shirt around the lower part of which was a wide belt in which he carried his hunting knife and tomahawk. His breeches were of fine doeskin, neatly fringed along the outer seams. His feet were clad in the customary frontier moccasins. Even in this rugged dress, Sevier's dignity and military bearing stood out. From his exploits along the Nolichucky River, he gained the life-long nickname of "Nolichucky Jack." Sevier and his fellow frontiersmen inevitably came into conflict with the Indians.

He was a man whose faults stand out glaringly in the records of some historians, but he was also the most dynamic character in the early history of the Smoky Mountain Country.

Life As It Was

The first settlers in East Tennessee, which is to say the first white residents of the state itself, were pioneers in more ways than one. They established the first church, the first institution of learning, and the second newspaper west of the Alleghenies. But in the beginning their means of survival were crude indeed. They had no clocks or watches, and determined the time of day by the shadow cast upon a homemade sundial. The time of night was reckoned by the position of the stars, when they could be seen. Months and years were measured in number of moons. The course, density, and velocity of the clouds helped them ascertain the temperature, weather in general being determined by the direction and velocity of the wind and the habits of the numerous wild birds and animals, which were an everyday part of their lives. To guide the planting and harvesting of their crops, they studied the growth of wild plants and vegetables.

The early homes were rough but sturdy; parts of some of them are still in existence. Usually containing only one room, they were built of logs hewn from the trees that had stood on the site of the cabin. The logs were fitted together by notches, and the cracks between them filled by daubing clay from nearby dirt banks. Above the single room was a loft for the older boys of the family. This was a typical abode of the poorer settlers; those of the more affluent were somewhat more elaborate, usually having two rooms on the ground floor, with an open hallway called a "dog trot" in between. Both rooms and hallway faced the front, with the hallway in some instances being enclosed from the weather. As prosperity increased, a porch of medium height was added to the front of the house, and a second floor with two rooms similar to those below.

The building was topped off with a single-gabled roof covered with hand-split shingles cut from short lengths of oak logs with a rough tool called a "frow." This was a blunt, scythe-like instrument with a thick edge, from which the expression "as dull as a frow" originated. At first the shingles were fastened in place with wooden pegs, later on by short, square-shaped nails. A huge stone chimney was at each end of the house, its bottom part spreading in a great bulge to accommodate the spacious fireplace inside. There were no windows at the ends of the house, in fact no room for them, but "porthole openings" were made in the front and rear walls. In later times, tiny windows were cut in the ends of the houses, just above the fireplace bulge. The kitchen projected at right angles to the building; and other rooms were added in this same fashion. Split-log puncheons were used to cover the floors in the earliest cabins, these later to be replaced by planks which, if more modern, were less durable.

The household utensils consisted of a Dutch oven, a skillet, and a pot. Wooden trenchers and dressed boards were used in place of dishes. Both cooking and eating were done beside the open hearth. A few slab benches and a rifle rack just about completed the house furnishings. The meat was deer, beef, pork, wild turkey, gray squirrels, and rabbits, whichever happened to be nearest the cabin at the moment. The vegetables were corn, beans, wheat (when it could be ground, as there were few mills for this purpose), potatoes, squash, pumpkins, cabbage, turnip greens; corn was grated in a hand mill and hominy made in a sort of block designed for this purpose. The fruits were apples, peaches, grapes, plums, muscadines, "sarviss berries," scuppernongs, huckleberries, raspberries, and that standby for the peerless cobbler pies of the region, wild blackberries. A kind of maple sugar was obtained from a local variety of the tree.

In the one-room cabins the entire family — and they were usually large in size; one family of my close relatives included seven brothers and seven sisters — ate, slept, and performed their ablutions, ofttimes to the embarrassment of visitors, who had to stay in the room and do likewise. The earlier settlers slept in their daytime clothes or underwear, usually several in one bed, thus having warmth in winter if not privacy. Baths were virtually unknown except in the creeks in summer, so body odors were the accepted accompaniment of the other familiar smells of the household. Later on baths were taken before the fireplace in the round washtubs, as hard for the average adult to get into as they were lacking in cleansing facilities. Strong laundry soap was used, which acted upon the skin something in the manner of fine sandpaper garnished with turpentine. Hot water, poured into the tub from the sizzling kettle at the fireplace, all too quickly cooled off. When the would-be bather had finished and by muscular manipulation managed to get out of the tub, he usually drenched the floor. Privies were more the exception than the rule.

As time went on, brick and stone began to be used in the building of the better houses. The roofs were made of smoother shingles, and shutters made their appearance on some windows, which now were often made of glass. Toward the end of the eighteenth century, the finest home in Tennessee was the Ramsay house near Knoxville. It was a large structure built of stone, with a deep basement, two tall stories, and an attic. The top of its tall chimney, as well as the corners and arches of the house, were of bluestone. The windows were long and narrow, and the house inside was ornately decorated and furnished. The walls were red granite.

The clothing of the men was made from animal skins or coarsely woven cloth, their fringed pockets and trousers and coonskin caps giving them an appearance as rugged as some of the animals they hunted. The social standing of the women could be judged by their garb — as indeed it can to some extent today. Linsey-woolsey, a fabric with a flax framework filled in with wool, was widely used by the poorer women. Some wore deerskins like those of their husbands. The linsey-woolsey, like cotton cloth later, was made at home by the women on their carding boards and spinning wheels. Tanning leather for use in shoes and other items grew to be a substantial home industry; even today, in the Great Smoky Mountains, there remain a few of the old tanning mills which made leather from animal hides by means of juice ground from the bark of trees. I recall that as a boy it was my lot to kill all the newborn bull calves from our dairy herd, and then skin them to get their hides. As a result, to this day I do not like veal.

Not all the clothes were made of animal skins, nor did all the women look like Daniel Boone's sister. As the settlers prospered, which they did very rapidly, their clothes caught up with their fortunes. Women began to don high heels, brocade, even silks and satins. Well-to-do men like John Sevier, James Robertson, and Evan Shelby when appearing at special occasions were clad in silk breeches and stockings, silk jackets, pumps, and knee buckles.

As to the custom of going without shoes, this legend which has sprung up about the uplands is as exaggerated as it is ridiculous. The skins of animals for use as shoes were plentiful, and in winter all the early settlers, with the possible exception of a few isolated, destitute cases, protected their feet just as they did their arms and legs. With the coming of spring it was another story. Any Yankee who has read Whittier's *The Barefoot Boy* should need no explanation of why folks like to go barefoot in the warm weather, even grown folks. I remember how difficult it was to wait until the coming of the balmy days when we youngsters could turn out in our naked feet to dash over the grass or through the hillside woods, stopping beside a brook to push our toes into the warming sands along the edge, then into the sparkling cool mountain waters. It was a joyful time and we went barefoot because we wanted to. When cool weather arrived in late fall, we donned our new shoes, ordered weeks before from the Sears, Roebuck catalog, and remained well shod all winter until spring came round again. So it was with my parents and grandparents.

The Tennessee-Carolina frontiersman, along with his plain, strict family life, also liked his fun. During ground-clearings, when all the neighbors gathered to root out trees and clean up the brush, a frolic was ordinarily held at night. Quiltings, spelling bees, house-raisings, corn-shuckings, flax-pullings, candy-pullings, box suppers, ice cream suppers, and square dances all brightened the strenuous hunting-farming routine of these pioneers. Hard cider and corn whiskey were the chief drinks on such occasions, although there were those with religious scruples who partook of neither. Later on, after iron rolls were introduced in the grinding of sorghum cane and horses used for power, the subsequent boiling down of the cane juice into molasses became the occasion for singing folk songs under the stars, dancing on the ground-up cane stalks, and playing running games in which, if a boy caught a girl, he could kiss her, much to the delight of the younger children.

Many social events were held at the numerous inns which dotted the trails leading from Virginia, Kentucky, and North Carolina into Tennessee. That the aftermath of such parties was not always unadulterated happiness may be surmised from the following advertisement placed in the Knoxville *Gazette* of January 16, 1793:

TAKE NOTICE ALL YE WHISKEY DRINKERS

That I will positively sue every person indebted
to me in twenty-one days from this date
if they do not make payment.

Benjamin White

The frontiersman was a man who could swear, shoot, fight, gamble, and drink. Most of them chewed tobacco — they often called it "eatin' terbaccer," supposedly because they swallowed some of the juice — , and a great number of the women either smoked a pipe or used snuff. The pipe-smoking on the distaff side has about died down by now, but the dipping of snuff is still prevalent among a lot of these Southern women, who regard it as no worse than smoking cigarettes. In fact, just about every country store in the Tennessee-Carolina uplands today has a large supply of several brands and sizes of snuff. It is understood that the big snuff company which supplies most of this "delicacy" has never failed to declare an annual dividend in all its long history.

II

John Sevier and the Indians

Peaceful pursuits were, by necessity, only a part-time activity of the pioneers. The East Tennessee uplands were on the ragged fringe of civilization, and behind, toward North Carolina and Virginia, there was little support against danger for all too many miles of unbroken wilderness.

A fact often lost sight of, however, is that the Indians showed friendliness in nearly every instance when they first came in contact with the white men. They even offered to share their lands with the pale-faced intruders. Whether this attitude would have remained constant or could have been sustained, it is impossible to say. Both whites and Indians contributed to the breaking of good faith. The invaders were not satisfied to remain in any Watauga or Carter's Valley. They looked with envious eyes upon the greater stretches of fertile land beyond, which still belonged to the Cherokees, and made no bones about their intentions of acquiring it. They steadily encroached upon the hunting grounds of the red men and made real peace impossible. War was inevitable. Treaties made by the whites were promptly broken by them, which caused the Indian to lose his respect for the white man's word. To add to the hopelessness of the situation, the Indians differed among themselves, every good hunting ground being claimed by several tribes.

Theodore Roosevelt, as a historian, was prejudiced against the Indians, but nevertheless had a realistic viewpoint. In his *The Winning of the West* he said of the Tennessee upland strife:

> . . . it could not be otherwise when brutal, reckless and lawless borderers, despising all men not their own color, were thrown in contact with savages who esteemed cruelty and treachery as the highest virtues, and rapine and murder as the worthiest of pursuits. It was inevitable too that the law-abiding people on both sides should be drawn into the conflict. . . . Mere outrages could be atoned for or settled; the question that lay at the root of our difficulties was that of the occupation of the land itself, and to this there could be no solution save war.

And so the war whoop rang through the land, across the upland forests and in the valleys. It brought terror even to hearts that had stoutly braved every hazard of the old country, and, thus far, of the new. In each cabin there was constant dread of the tomahawk and scalping knife. No thicket could be passed without fear that behind it lurked a red skin. Once aroused, the Indians stopped at nothing. Even the Cherokees, who had taken possession of East Tennessee about 1623 and had held it ever since, who were so far above other tribes in their civilization that they had a written language of their own, were little different from other Indians in their depredations. If they could not win victory in open fighting, then treacherous ambush, the torch, and the midnight shriek of butchery followed. Homes were destroyed and no record left.

The white men were on perpetual alert, working, hunting,

fishing, farming, worshiping, and sleeping always with their long rifles at hand and their long knives to back them up. No less did the women stand guard. They became skillful in the use of deadly weapons. Near the present town of Maryville, Miss Mary McEwan — later to become Mrs. Samuel Doak, wife of the educator — was in her home when the Indians attacked. Quickly she turned to molding bullets for the men defending the house. An Indian bullet whizzed through the room, bounced off the wall, and fell in the floor. Calmly she picked it up, remolded it, and gave it to one of the men, saying: "Here, give it back to them!"

But if the whites feared the Indians, the latter, in turn, were up against a tough breed of men. Anglo-Saxon, mostly Highlanders, they had already fought their way through the valleys of Virginia or the mountains of North Carolina — Yorkshiremen who used such words as *wrassle, dang, by gum, agin, this-a-way, consarned, jist,* and *yaller,* words which live in these mountains today; and Scots-Irish who had come by way of Pennsylvania from the four counties of Northern Ireland, where their ancestors had settled after the reign of Queen Elizabeth, and who brought with them the Elizabethan speech still to be heard in the Smoky Mountain Country. About them, John Trotwood Moore wrote:

> If abused, they fight; if their rights are infringed, they rebel; if forced, they strike; and if their liberties are threatened, they murder. . . . They eat meat and their bread is always hot.

Because he had to fight so much in his lifetime, the pioneer settler considered himself a soldier. His rifle, knife, and horse could all be turned to war at a moment's notice. Each had his home, his family, and his leader, and he held these above all other things except Almighty God. According to Lyman Draper, who collected many priceless documents of the period:

> In fighting, everyone fought for himself, officers as well as men. The best officers were those who fought best; as among the Indians, the officers were leaders rather than commanders. In fighting, it was always expected that the officers would lead on; any failure to do so would be regarded as cowardice, and the officers cashiered not by court martial but by acclamation.

Such were the men who chose John Sevier as their leader in war and peace. They considered it an honor to go wherever and whenever he called. The long record of unbroken popular devotion to Sevier exceeded that of any other leader of his day. After settling at Watauga in 1772, he was for the next twenty years almost constantly fighting the Indians or planning campaigns against them. As soon as the Cherokees started their atrocities, he gathered the men of the settlements around him and took after the marauders. He did great damage, burning and destroying Indian towns in an early "scorched earth" policy, yet sustaining little injury to his own men. He started and brought to a successful and complete end more Indian wars than any man in history, with the least damage to his own side. His plan was one of aggression. If possible, he never waited until the Indians attacked, but went after them first. His strategy of swift movement on horses and his tactics of surprise rank with those of Forrest and Morgan, two better-known later fighters in this region.

When the Revolution broke out, Sevier was forced not only to continue his fights against the Indians, but to take on the British as well. He went about these duties saddened by the death of his first wife, who had borne him ten children. But some years later, defending Fort Caswell against an Indian siege, he anxiously watched while a tall, graceful girl, who had strayed outside the fort, ran for the stockade closely pursued by Indian braves. The men inside could not shoot for fear of hitting her. As they held their breath, they saw her outrun the red men and jump over the stockade just in time — into the arms of John Sevier. Not long afterward, she and Sevier were married; and in time she bore him eight children. Of his eighteen in all, ten were stalwart boys who in later years formed a tacit bodyguard for their famous father. "Bonnie Kate," as his second wife was called, must have been a good-natured spouse, for Sevier had a habit of bringing home large groups of friends for dinner without advance warning. Once when he had captured thirty Indians and did not know what to do with them, he brought them to his home. They liked the place so well they would not leave, and eventually built themselves cabins and settled in the neighborhood.

The crafty Sevier utilized the services of friendly Indians, of whom there were a great many, to outsmart the hostile ones. This practice, plus his courage, his knowledge of the woods, and his forthrightness, helped to account for his success. He never believed in the promises of an Indian and was convinced that the only good ones were dead ones. He used extreme caution when not in sight of the enemy, but was recklessly daring in their presence. Sometimes he was cruel. On one expedition, near the present town of Tellico Plains, he and his men captured several chiefs and bound them hand and foot, placing them in a room under guard. While Sevier was out of the room, one of his troops, maddened by the massacre of his whole family a few days before, fell upon the defenseless chiefs with a tomahawk and killed them in cold blood. Sevier reprimanded the soldier, but his men taking the side of the slayer, he did no more. This was the blackest mark on Sevier's generally superb record.

Probably his greatest single achievement was the battle of King's Mountain, in North Carolina, an engagement which marked the turning point of the American Revolution. One story of this battle I have from my grandfather, whose grandfather in turn fought in this battle as a captain under Sevier, and who passed his account of it down by word of mouth.

Sevier, who had been made a colonel, was summoned with his long-riflemen to help drive the British Colonel Patrick Ferguson and his troops from the strategic mountain. Ferguson was a brave, left-handed firearms expert, a favorite in the British Army. Ensconced on the mountain, he boasted that "all the rebels in Hell and outside can't drive me from it."

Gathering his men almost overnight, Sevier made a quick march to King's Mountain. Just before arriving there, he stopped his force of several hundred and told them that anyone who wished to could back out. All those so desiring had only to step three paces to the rear. No one made a move.

"You understand," said Sevier. "Why don't you move?"

"Because," one of his men replied, "We can't move any way but forward."

The Americans under Colonels Sevier, Campbell, and Shelby surrounded the mountain and started the advance upward. There was not a regular-army soldier in the entire force. Suddenly they were met by a withering fire from the well-trained British regulars. The frontiersmen fell back, rallied, and then reverted to their tactics of the woods. Individually, in Indian fashion, they fought from tree to tree. Each man was on his own, officers included. Each man knew what to do and went at it in fierce determination born of many a skirmish with the red men of the forests. One of Ferguson's officers said later that Sevier's long-riflemen were "the most powerful-looking men I ever beheld, tall, raw-boned and sinewy, like so many devils from the infernal regions." But they were not infallible. Numbers of them started to retreat in the face of the hot fire from the breech-loading rifles which Ferguson himself had invented. Sevier rode after his men and persuaded them to return. Hand-to-hand fighting followed. Within twenty minutes from its beginning, the battle of King's Mountain was over. The mountain no longer belonged to the king. Ferguson himself was killed, a third of his force of eleven hundred killed or wounded, and the rest taken prisoner. The Americans lost twenty-eight killed, sixty wounded. Of the seven Seviers who fought in the battle, one, Robert, a brother of John, was killed. The quickness and decisiveness with which this battle was brought to a close was almost phenomenal in military annals; and when it was over, the mountain men of Tennessee and North Carolina quietly scattered and hurried to their homes in the Smokies to see if the Cherokees had scalped their women and children while they were away.

After his triumphant return from the battle, Sevier spent the next several years wiping out the remainder of the hostile Indians from Virginia to Georgia. In all he fought thirty-five battles with the red men and won thirty-five victories. He was never even wounded, the closest he came to dangerous injury being when he fought hand-to-hand with the great chief Dragging Canoe and had a lock of his hair shot off. Only once did the government pay his men for their services; the rest of the time Sevier paid them out of his own pocket. As a consequence, he died a poor man.

In 1784, Sevier was elected governor of the State of Franklin, a new commonwealth carved out of the land around Watauga. At first the 100,000 people of this territory had sought annexation to North Carolina, but the latter, fearing additional federal taxes if enlarged, would have none of it. So the new state was formed, taking its name from Benjamin Franklin. Then North Carolina wanted the "state" back, but this time it refused. In fact, Franklin kept on being a state for four years, with John Sevier as governor, with its own laws, courts, and taxes. Sevier was accused of treason by North Carolina, arrested, and taken there for trial, but escaped. Finally, in 1790, the territory of the State of Franklin was ceded to the federal government and William Blount was made its territorial governor. Sevier became a brigadier general in the United States Army.

Competing also for the brigadier generalship was one Andrew Jackson, who was to become a bitter enemy of Sevier. (Both men have been accused by historians of land speculation, but considering the vagueness of the evidence and the fact that there was little else to speculate in, the claim against them is not a strong one.) Sevier became the first governor of the state of Tennessee when it was formed in 1796. He served three terms, then, after a brief interlude, three more. In his campaign for the fourth term, Sevier was opposed by Jackson. Results: Sevier 6786 votes, Jackson 4923. Soon afterwards, the two famous warriors met on the street in Knoxville, and Sevier accused Jackson of "running off with another man's wife." Jackson challenged Sevier to a duel. The latter suggested that it be fought in Kentucky instead of in Tennessee. Jackson called Sevier a coward. The argument over technicalities continued between the two and their seconds until one day they met again on a trail. Both pulled pistols, glared, cursed, but no fight ensued. Some said that Jackson feared the consequences from Sevier's ten sons if he killed him. Others believed that it was simply a draw between great fighters, with neither rising to the advantage.

From 1811 to 1815 Sevier was a member of Congress from Tennessee, retiring afterward to live in his large farmhouse just outside of Knoxville, where, in sight of his beloved Smokies, he entertained friends and men of high rank from both home and abroad. He died in 1815 while on a mission to the Creek Indians in Georgia, the personification of the finest type of frontiersman not only of early Tennessee but of the whole nation's advance westward. He guided a tiny, insecure outpost to full-fledged statehood. Brave, steadfast, and statesmanlike, as rugged as the Smoky Mountains, Sevier was the product of his era.

The Terrible Harps

Celebrated in crime have been Jesse James of Missouri, Billy the Kid of Texas, and many others, but for some reason, perhaps because it was felt the less said about the heinous pair the better, little has been written about East Tennessee's Harp brothers. Yet these two, with their mockingly celestial names, were probably more bloody and took more sadistic toll of human life than the others.

In 1797 there came to Knox County two brothers, Micajah and Wiley Harp, bringing with them two women who regularly bore illegitimate children — whom the fathers promptly dispatched. The couples settled near the town of Knoxville and soon were stealing hogs and sheep. This was not considered so bad, but then their thieving turned to horses, a capital offense in those days. The Harps fled from the vigorous arm of the frontier law and took to the woods, where they and their women lived like hunted animals, and bred and subsisted in much the same manner.

About this time — as was later told by Micajah Harp, the elder, who, being much larger in physique, came to be known as the "Big Harp" — the two brothers turned against humanity. They determined to kill all the people they could before they themselves were caught and done away with. Seeing a man with a sack of corn on his back going to mill, they murdered him and took the corn for food. A few days later, they killed another man near Knoxville, and in a crude effort to eliminate the evidence, ripped his body open with knives, took out the insides, filled the torso with stones, and threw it into the Holston River.

By this time the citizenry were thoroughly aroused, and organized posses to catch them; but the Harps were too evasive. They proceeded to murder another hapless traveler. The posses in pursuit became small armies, and chased them into the wilderness along the Tennessee-Kentucky line. The Harps and their women hid out in a wild declivity known as Cave-In-Rock, and here they stayed for a long time, making it their headquarters and faring forth and committing murders on virtually a wholesale basis, most of their depredations being in what is now Union and Claiborne counties. Eventually other criminals began to flock to this hideout, until so many came they outnumbered the Harps. One day a canoe containing two hunters came down the river. The Harps spied them, and by subterfuge succeeded in getting them to row over to the shore. Then the Harps grabbed the unfortunate pair, forced them blindfolded onto a horse, and drove the horse and riders off a five hundred-foot cliff, to a crushing death on the rocks below. This inhuman feat outraged even the other criminals at Cave-In-Rock, so they demanded that the Harps depart.

On their way toward Knoxville, the Harps stopped at the farmhouse of a Mr. Langford early one morning, ate breakfast, quarreled with him over the price, and ended up by murdering him and hiding his body in the woods. This time they were caught by a posse and placed in jail. But with the coming of night, the murderers promptly escaped. The next morning they chanced to come upon a small Negro boy, whom they killed by beating his brains out against a tree. Stopping at the home of a farmer named Stegall, they asked for breakfast. While Mrs. Stegall was preparing it, her baby in its crib began to cry — but not for long. When she returned to the room to invite the Harps to eat, she screamed in horror: her baby's throat had been cut as it cried in the crib. To stop the mother's cries, the Harps stabbed her to death with a butcher knife, and, after they had leisurely eaten their breakfast, they set fire to the house and took their leave.

But this time their woodland lair was not so encompassing. Led by the husband of the murdered woman, a band of grim, determined men on horseback pursued the Harps day and night. Finally one of them, Thomas Leiper, caught up with the Big Harp and shot him. The murderer fell against a log and lay there. Leiper approached cautiously, his gun drawn. But the human fiend was helpless, being badly wounded. He could talk, however, and strangely enough showed no fear. He told Leiper how he and his brother had turned against mankind, knowing that their murderous deeds would lead some day to their own deaths. Asked if he regretted any of his crimes, the Big Harp said only one had bothered his conscience any. That was the murder of his own child, whom he had killed when it cried and vexed him.

As he lay there talking to Leiper, Harp saw others of the posse arrive, among them Stegall, the husband of the murdered mother. Unable to restrain himself, Stegall sprang from his horse and advanced upon the Big Harp with a butcher knife. The latter calmly offered no resistance, and as Stegall in his mad rage began hacking at the murderer's head, Harp glared and said:

"You're a poor butcher. Cut and be damned!"

Soon afterward, the Harps' women were captured. They denied that they had taken any part in the crimes, and said they had stayed with the Harps only because they were afraid that if they tried to leave them, they would be killed. The women were released; but the head of the Big Harp was placed high in the forks of a tree beside a main trail, there to remain as a ghastly reminder for several years.

The Little Harp had escaped. It was now 1802, five years after the fanatical brothers had embarked on their orgy of blood. Three years later, along the famous trail known as the Natchez Trace, which led from Nashville to the Mississippi town, a reward was offered for the head of a certain dangerous criminal. Soon afterward, a man appeared carrying the head wrapped in blue clay. As he tried to claim the reward, he was recognized as the Little Harp by a man who had pursued him years before, and was hanged on the spot.

It has been estimated that the Terrible Harps, in their career of horror, committed thirty murders — a record of which Tennessee is not proud.

Jackson and the Cherokees

When Tennessee became a state in 1796 and Sevier was elected its first governor, William Blount was sent to the United States Senate, and Andrew Jackson to Congress.

The senatorial record of Blount is hardly a credit to the annals of Tennessee, for he was expelled from that body almost as soon as he was seated. The reason was his involvement in a major scandal, that of participating in the war then growing between England and France. Blount, being a strong Tory, sympathized with Britain, and cooked up a scheme of recruiting partisan fighters in Tennessee to raid the French territories of Louisiana and Florida. Unfortunately for him, he made the mistake of setting forth these plans in a letter to James Carey of Tellico Blockhouse. The letter, which specifically asked for help from the East Tennessee Cherokees,* fell into the hands of enemies of Blount and was published in the newspapers. The new senator was expelled on July 8, 1797, a resolution for an impeachment trial barely falling through because of his strong support among western congressmen.

But the star of Andrew Jackson, who resigned from the House and ran successfully for Blount's seat, rose out of the Tennessee wilds to high ascendancy. In looks and tempera-

---

* Appointed as federal Indian agent to the Cherokees in 1801 was a man by the name of Return Jonathan Meigs. How he received this unusual name is worth recalling. His father, while young, paid constant court to a young Quakeress near his home in Middletown, Connecticut, but was repeatedly rejected by her with the words: "Nay, Jonathan, I respect thee much but I cannot marry thee." But on his last visit, as he slowly and sadly mounted his horse for the final departure, he saw to his surprise the relenting lady beckoning to him and calling: "Return, Jonathan! Return, Jonathan!" Feeling that these words were the sweetest he ever heard, he gave them as a name to their first-born son.

ment he represented the wildness of the new west as much as a movie hero now does. A lean, skinny man with sandy hair and blue eyes that looked as if they were sighting over a rifle barrel, this fiery figure dominated the affairs of Tennessee for so many years that some historians of the period are prone to ignore the state and concentrate on the man. It is not recorded that Jackson did anything outstanding in either chamber of Congress, and he resigned in 1799 to accept the post of judge of the Tennessee Superior Court of Law and Equity, being appointed to the position by John Sevier. The next year, Jackson again changed jobs, this time defeating Sevier himself in an election for the position of major general of the Tennessee Militia. The outcome of this contest was not so important as the feud which developed between Jackson and Sevier, a feud which was to rock the politics of the state for years. One result of it was a legislative investigation, in 1803, of Sevier for complicity in a big land fraud. Despite the support of Jackson, the investigation failed.

The War of 1812 did much to increase Jackson's political stature. He organized a horde of volunteers to march against the British — whom he hated — , and though there was no fighting immediately, he did win the strong devotion of his troops, a sentiment which was to be of much help to him in later years. The Creek Indians went on the warpath, and Jackson, with a volunteer force of whites and Cherokees, subdued them at the battle of Horse Shoe Bend. But it was his epochal victory of Tennessee and Carolina squirrel hunters over the trained British at the battle of New Orleans in 1814 which catapulted him into national prominence. By the early 1820's he was being groomed for President, and in the election of 1828 entered the White House. Though a landowner, he became the champion of the average man. He smashed the

Bank of the United States, upheld Peggy O'Neill, feuded with John C. Calhoun, and presided over the famous Kitchen Cabinet. He even named his successor, Martin van Buren; and another of his followers, James K. Polk, a fellow-Tennessean and an often underrated statesman, was elected President in 1844. Through all of this period, Jackson largely controlled Tennessee politics as well as national affairs. In fact, his sway over the state was interrupted only once, when his protégé, Governor Sam Houston, abruptly resigned and departed to Texas when he found that his wife didn't love him.

One of the worst blots on Jackson's record was his treatment of the Cherokee Indians. Chief Junaluska of their number, for whom a beautiful North Carolina lake was named, was among the Cherokees who fought with Jackson against the Creeks at Horseshoe Bend. Years afterward, this chief remarked: "If I had known Jackson would have driven us from our homes, I would have killed him that day at Horseshoe Bend."

To understand the situation, it is necessary to realize that by 1830 the Cherokees of East Tennessee, western North Carolina, and North Georgia had nearly all become prosperous farmers, some of them owning slaves. They even had their own alphabet, invented by a part-Cherokee named Sequoyah, known by the white people as George Guess. This remarkable individual, who could not speak, read, or write English but who had been told about the Moses in the Bible who "wrote on stones," was interested in drawing and designing, and eventually became fascinated by the white man's alphabet, which "wrote down what was passing in their minds so it would keep." He went to work to create a Cherokee alphabet, and for ten years labored patiently at this task, often amid the jeers of skeptical associates — and even of his wife, who in disgust threw the results of his first two years' work into the fire. Stoically, he started all over, and when he finally succeeded in creating an alphabet with eighty-six characters, he was accorded the proverbial recognition given those who reach success after being scorned.

A printing press was purchased in Boston and brought south, and the printing of the new Cherokee language began. In 1828 a newspaper, the Cherokee *Phoenix,* was started, printed partly in Cherokee and partly in English. Edited and published by Isaac Harris and John F. Wheeler, the paper lasted for several years. It was hailed as an innovation in many parts of the world, and was exchanged, for instance, with the *Times* of London. Parts of the Bible were translated into the new Cherokee. Young Indians learned to write their own language in two days. The Cherokees thus became the only American Indians to have a printed language, the first to have their own newspaper, the first to print their own books. It may fittingly be pointed out that they also had the first regularly elected government of any Indian nation, modeled after our own and including a written constitution and trial by jury. Sequoyah was honored far and wide. He became the beneficiary of the only literary pension granted by the United States Government, and received a medal from Congress. After he had become old, he continued his pioneering by going in search of what was said to be a lost band of Cherokees in the Far West. He died at San Fernando, Mexico, in 1843, but his name is perpetuated in the giant trees of the Pacific Coast.

Even a cursory examination of the background gives justification for the accusation by the historian James Mooney that Jackson was "an Indian hater." Current perspective does not justify Old Hickory's harsh attitude, despite his early background of hardships in the wilderness and his known tendency to be extreme in his feelings; but Jackson, as usual, was justified in his own mind. Besides his intimate recollections of the horrors of Indian warfare, he was a politician. Before his first election to the presidency, he had promised the Georgia delegation in Congress that they would have his help when he was in the White House. For this promise, they exacted bitter toll. After Jackson's request for an Indian removal bill, and its passage by Congress in 1830, Georgia annexed all Cherokee lands, and the Indians' laws were declared null and void. The Cherokees were forbidden to meet or hold council together. The predatory whites began to move onto the red men's land and take their property — all with the help and connivance of the Georgia state government. Contracts between Cherokee and white were declared unenforceable, and personal debts to the hitherto-prospering Indians were canceled. In this conservative section of the nation, one day to be called the Bible belt, a great lottery was set up to distribute the Cherokee land. It was cut up into sections of one hundred sixty acres each, and every white citizen of Georgia received a free ticket. When he "won" his land, he moved onto it, shoving the poor Cherokee off.*

Jackson's mind brooked few compromises and he was con-

* The Reverend H. Ruffner, president of Washington College, while on a tour from Virginia to Tennessee in July, 1838, made the following note: "No wonder that the Cherokee loved his fatherland, when it was so lovely in itself, and was moreover the seat of his tribe and the dwelling place of his fathers, from time beyond the reach of tradition. All that can attach to the earth, attached him to the woody hills, the rich vales and the clear fountains of this beautiful region. No wonder that this, the most civilized of the Indian tribes, clung with fond affection to the delightful home which God had given them; but the white man coveted it and would have it because he could take it by force."

vinced that white and red man could not live together. An appeal to him brought only the answer that nothing could be done unless the Indians consented to be removed to the West; there they would dwell in "a happy land beyond the setting sun." Alas, many of them were to die en route and dwell only beneath that land. Two Christian missionaries who had sided with the Cherokees, most of whom had now become Christians themselves, were thrown into prison. Their case was taken all the way to the United States Supreme Court, where Chief Justice John Marshall and the majority members reversed the state courts and ordered the missionaries released. Of this famous decision, Jackson is said to have remarked: "John Marshall has made his decision; now let him enforce it." Popular sentiment alone, however, was soon enough to effect the release of the men.

John Ross, principal chief of the Cherokees from 1828 until he died in 1866, and whose home still stands at Rossville, Georgia, near Chattanooga, strove valiantly until the end against the preparations of the government to remove his people. Ross was part Scottish as well as Cherokee, and was as stubborn as that other part-Scot, Andrew Jackson — but without the resources of the federal government behind him. During one of the painful stages of the Cherokee removal, John Howard Payne, author of *Home Sweet Home,* was visiting Ross, a lifelong friend. Evening had come and the two men were seated beside the fireplace chatting, when suddenly the door burst open and eight Georgia militiamen strode in. They summarily arrested Ross and Payne and took them away on horseback. It was to be an all-night journey, and rain was falling. As midnight approached, Payne's escort became drowsy. To keep himself awake, the soldier began to sing *Home Sweet Home.*

"Little did I ever expect to hear that song under such sad circumstances," said Payne.

"Reckon not," replied the soldier. "But it's a good song."

"Do you know who wrote it?" asked Payne.

"No, do you?"

"Yes, I wrote it."

"Like hell you did!" snorted the soldier. "You might tell that to some people, but not to me. All right, if you made up that song, say every word of it or I'll bounce you off your horse."

In a slow, solemn tone, Payne spoke — and then sang — the song, filling the dark, woody trail with the melancholy melody.

"By God, you did write it!" said the soldier, plainly touched. He thought for a minute, then said that the prisoners would not go to jail if he could help it.

The next day Payne and Ross were released.

Andrew Ross, brother of John, led a small faction of the Indians to Washington to make a separate treaty calling for the removal of the Cherokees. The treaty, repudiated by the rest of the tribe, provided that the Indians would migrate to the West within two years; and it was passed by the Senate in 1836 by a majority of one vote. Henry Clay thundered against it, as did Edward Everett of Massachusetts. Courageous Congressman David Crockett of Tennessee broke with Jackson on the issue and knowingly sacrificed his political career in the fight, stating that he could not conscientiously support such a measure. It is significant that an old Indian fighter like Crockett would take such a stand on the question, for he too knew the Cherokees well. Not long after this, he went to Texas, and subsequently to his heroic death as the last man at the Alamo. Before leaving, he told a large local audience:

"Folks, I'm going to Texas. The rest of you can go to hell!"

So the long march along the "Trail of Tears" began. About fifteen thousand Cherokees were rounded up by General John S. Wool, later by General Winfield Scott. After a sad final meeting with their chieftain, John Ross, near Charleston in the foothills of the Smokies, at which they still affirmed their rights to the land, the Indians started on the trip west. They traveled by barge on the rivers, and on foot. The trek was made in a winter which proved to be unusually severe, and many of the squaws and especially the children soon became ill. The exposure, the exhaustion of the hard trip, and the lack of adequate medical care quickly thinned the ranks of the unfortunate Indians. By the time they had reached the Oklahoma territory designated for them, almost a third had died. Their path has aptly been designated "the saddest trail in American history."

But not even doughty General Scott could round up all the Cherokees. The Great Smoky Mountains held many a secluded hiding place among its coves and peaks, and despite the systematic efforts of Scott's troops, about fifteen hundred of the Indians hid out here. They placed themselves under the leadership of Chief Utsala ("the Lichen"), most of them living near the headwaters of the Ocona-Luftee and Tuckasegee rivers. General Scott, prodded by Washington, finally sent two regiments to rout these red men out. What happened thereafter is the subject of an impressive outdoor historical drama which was presented at Cherokee, North Carolina, in the summers of 1950 and 1951, and which bade fair to continue for some time. The play is entitled *Unto These Hills* and portrays with reasonable accuracy the story of one Cherokee who stayed behind.

It was my good fortune to witness one of the performances.

The setting is part of the Qualla Reservation, where the only remaining band of Cherokee Indians in the eastern United States lives, and where the Indian children learn to read and write Cherokee as well as English. Produced by the Cherokee Historical Association, the play had in its cast one hundred twenty Indians and some white members of the Carolina Playmakers of the University of North Carolina. In a strikingly natural outdoor theater on the mountainside, surrounded by hemlock, maple, rhododendron, laurel, flame azalea, and dogwood, with the Smokies for a backdrop and the azure sky for a ceiling, I saw a moving portrayal of the tragedy of the Cherokees. Tsali, or Charley, was one of the members of the tribe who hid behind. He lived in a little cabin on the line between Tennessee and North Carolina, where he was finally discovered by the troops of General Scott. With his wife, brother, and two sons, Tsali was started toward the government stockade at Calhoun, Tennessee, prior to being sent west. The mountain trail was steep and the wife of Tsali did not feel well. Several times she lagged, which did not please the soldier who accompanied her. He began to prod her with his bayonet. Tsali grew more and more angry at this treatment, until finally, after she was nudged with an extremely sharp thrust, he could stand it no longer. He pounced upon the soldier, took his bayonet away, and killed him. Tsali's brother then jumped upon another soldier and killed him. Before the other astonished troopers could collect their wits, Tsali and his family had fled over the mountains. When General Scott heard of the incident, he was outraged. Chagrined anyway over his failure to find all the Indians, he sent word through an emissary that if Tsali would surrender and be punished, Scott would leave the rest of Utsala's refugees alone, and try to arrange permission for them to stay perma-

nently in the mountains. Tsali hesitated. He knew what surrender meant. Finally, for the sake of his fellow Cherokees,
he and his sons and brother came down and gave themselves
up. They were lined up and shot, all except the youngest son
of Tsali. But the Cherokees were allowed to remain in the
Smokies, where they live until this day.

III

Brother against Brother

In the period preceding the Civil War, Tennessee was tranquil. It had furnished Andrew Jackson, Sam Houston, and James K. Polk to the new nation, and as far as statesmen were concerned had more than done its share. But neither in its contributions nor characteristics was the state united. Its three grand divisions, East, Middle, and West Tennessee, stood out in such sharply individual relief that many residents wondered why, in the first place, the founding fathers had not made three states instead of one out of this heterogeneous parallelogram.

The two westward sections were of the Old South and its legendary ways. East Tennessee, like its mother state of North Carolina across the mountains, was a sort of little world in itself, a unique entity that was to retain this quality come Grant or Longstreet. It did not possess many slaves; in the Smoky Mountain region, the ratio was about one to every twelve whites, while in the other major parts of the state it was approximately one to two. There were many reasons for this, the principal one being economic. The mountains and the small valleys were not conducive to the extensive use of slaves, the little farms usually being worked without difficulty by their white owners.* In the eastern lowlands a few large landowners had several slaves tilling their fertile acres, but there is record of only one East Tennessean who owned more than a hundred slaves. This number and more were commonplace among many of the individual plantation owners of the middle and western parts of the state.

Not that the East Tennesseans liked Negroes. Most of them did not. The tenant workers feared that if the slaves were freed they would become successful competitors for the jobs of the poor-whites. The position of the landowners has been set forth; they held no strong moral feelings about the black race one way or the other. Some of the Northern abolitionist movements worked their way into these mountains to a slight extent. But mostly it was a simple matter of expediency. They just did not need slaves so much. Though the institution of slavery had existed here since the Negroes were first brought from Africa, the use of slaves had grown much faster in other parts of the South than in East Tennessee. This section of the state, while being the oldest, was more isolated by its mountains and retarded by its traditions and did not change as fast as did its sister sections.

Early Emancipators

Knoxville seems to have been the seat of early attempts at freeing the slaves. Back in 1797 the Knoxville *Gazette* had,

---

* Its white men were strong, and at least one of them was powerful big. He was Miles Darden, who was born in North Carolina but died in East Tennessee in 1857. At his death he reportedly weighed over 1000 pounds, and had been active until four years before. It took 13½ yards of cloth to make him a coat, his coffin was 8 feet long, 35 inches deep, 32 inches across the head, 18 inches across the feet. Some of his clothes are on view at the Tennessee Historical Society building in Nashville.

in response to urgings that the state abolish slavery, advocated that an abolition society be formed. In 1815 the Tennessee Manumission Society was organized at Lost Creek Meeting House in nearby Jefferson County by some Quakers and Covenanters, each of whom agreed to place in front of his house a sign which read: *Freedom is the natural right of all men.* An active member was one Elihu Embree, who, although an owner of slaves, started in the 1820's the first emancipation newspaper in the United States, the *Manumission Intelligencer,* a weekly which was later converted to the monthly *Emancipator.* Other such groups were soon formed in the region; and by 1827 East Tennessee had one-fifth of the abolition societies in the United States, with about the same proportion of membership.

Chief among the early opponents of slavery were the preachers. They had always opposed the institution, but the pastors of the Smoky Mountain Country were unusually vocal in their condemnation. None, however, reached the fanatic heights of a Henry Ward Beecher or Wendell Phillips; they were content to urge a gradual and reasonable elimination of the long-established black bondage, without violence. That their first earthly loyalty in this respect was to their native section was borne out, however, when the Methodists, Baptists, and Presbyterians later split wide open over the slavery question and formed Southern branches of their churches, some of which still exist. This schism of the churches is bound to have contributed markedly to the separation of the Southern states from the Union.

Reverend John Rankin of Jefferson County, a Presbyterian, was one of the milder early abolitionists. He moved to Ohio, but reported that there he found it "more dangerous to give an abolition speech than it had been in the South because greed had taken the place of justice"; and the Northern people, he said, wanted more than just freedom of the slaves. They had come to covet the spoils of war. Rankin wisely advocated the abolition of slavery by government purchase of the slaves, since they were a vital capital asset of the South and their sudden loss to the owners would represent a major economic disaster unless compensation in some form were forthcoming. This theory has grown in acceptance by historians as having offered the best possible substitute for the War between the States. When war did come, Rankin, a native East Tennessean, gave eight sons and one grandson to the Union armies. In his own house he is said to have sheltered Eliza Harris, the escaped slave of *Uncle Tom's Cabin*.

(There is a story told about one of the ministers of this period, who grew more and more skeptical of the religious devotion of his congregation in view of the gathering political storm. One morning he wound up his service by saying: "Next Sunday I am going to preach on the subject of liars. In this connection, as a preparation for my discourse, I should like you all to read the seventeenth chapter of *Mark*." On the following Sunday, the preacher rose and said: "Now then, all of you who have done as I requested and read the seventeenth chapter of *Mark*, please raise your hands." Nearly every hand in the congregation went up. Said the preacher: "You are the very people I want to talk to. There is no seventeenth chapter of *Mark*.")

The freeing of slaves in East Tennessee was a common practice long before Abraham Lincoln issued his Emancipation Proclamation.* But the process was not as simple a matter as

---

* An amendment to the Tennessee constitution providing for immediate emancipation was adopted in February, 1865, almost a year before the Thirteenth Amendment was added to the national constitution.

one might think. The law made it mandatory that any owner who wished to set his slaves free should petition the courts for permission to do so, and then furnish bond in order that the Negroes not become public charges, as they were often apt to. Despite the taunts of the abolitionists that emancipation was simply a moral question, the poor, freed slave had to be cared for. He was often worse than the Prisoner of Chillon, who stayed in his bondage so long that he returned to it even after he was freed. It is an established fact that many slaves did not wish to leave their owners, many never left them even after emancipation, while others returned to their former masters after sampling some of their new freedom.

Mrs. Jane Boren of East Tennessee freed a slave named Adam, then gave him, as *his* personal slave during his lifetime, his own daughter, Caroline. Mrs. Boren's will provided that with Adam's passing, Caroline would become free. To complicate matters more, both the father and daughter were given, as *their* slave, a Negro boy. To all three of these, Mrs. Boren bequeathed "one milk can, 20 bushels of corn, 10 bushels of wheat, three Bacon Hogs, three common bed quilts and one blanket."

The Unpopular War

In the presidential election of 1860, John Bell, a native Tennessean, was nominated as the candidate of the Constitutional Union Party, which strove to conciliate the radical factions and to prevent secession and preserve the Union. Led by the Union sympathizers of East Tennessee, Bell received the electoral votes of the state as well as those of Virginia

and Kentucky. This split with the supporters of the Democratic nominee, moderate Stephen A. Douglas, whose election
might well have averted the Civil War, helped give the national victory to Abraham Lincoln, although he did not get
a single vote in Tennessee. The attitude of the Smoky Mountain section was not anti-Lincoln or anti-Union, however. It
might be summed up in the words of Colonel S. R. Rodgers,
who was present at one of the ante-bellum conventions and
was asked to speak. Said he: "I am in favor of staying where
we are, in the Union, and in favor of doing nothing but
' holding plumb still.' "

However, there existed an entirely different situation at
Charleston, South Carolina. Fort Sumter's shots were heard
round the South with sadness and alarm. Along with its sister
states, against whom no Lincoln or Union or anything else
could induce it to make war, Tennessee, under the leadership
of its excitable governor Isham G. Harris, voted to secede, the
last of the states to do so. East Tennessee, however, voted by a
majority of 18,000 to stay with the Union. Senator Andrew
Johnson, who some years before had tried, almost successfully, to form a new state out of his homeland of East Tennessee, now tried again. But before he could get much support, Confederate troops had overrun the mountain country.
In spite of this, many of the men began to train for the
Union Army. In Blount County, for instance, companies of
"home guards" were formed, these actually being Union
sympathizers. A common sight was a train bearing Confederate soldiers passing through a town of this section and
being cheered by one faction, while an equal number of the
opposing side sulked within their homes and uttered threats
against the "uprising." One body of "Yankee followers"
could hardly be restrained from marching on Knoxville and

running "all the damned rebels out of the place." These rebels, however, shouted to their friends and brothers on the other side that it would not be long before the Confederates would be quaffing champagne in New York City.

In Washington, Tennessee's Andrew Johnson worked for days upon the most important speech of his career. When he arose to give it, he knowingly took his political life in his hands. He said of the Union: "I intend to cling to it as a ship-wrecked mariner clings to the last plank when the night and the tempest close around him. It is the last hope of human freedom." On the other hand, such eloquent Southern orators as Landon C. Haynes pleaded for adherence to the cause of the South. Haynes told a Knoxville audience that Tennessee's union with the Southern states was "natural and inseparable and the unalterable condition of her present and future safety, prosperity and independence." Also in Knoxville, the fiery Parson Brownlow, after printing what the Confederates considered "treasonable articles" in his newspaper, fled to Sevier County, where he was hidden by friends in the Smokies until his exile to the North. For some yet unexplained reason, most of the women of East Tennessee did not go along with their Unionist husbands in their beliefs and actions. A great number of the feminine side fervently embraced the cause of the South and stormed at their husbands, brothers, sons, and fathers until often they yielded before the domestic on-slaught and took up arms for the Confederacy. Many Union sympathizers fled to the more neutral state of Kentucky, where they eventually got into the Northern armies and re-turned to fight their brothers in East Tennessee and western North Carolina.

The most vivid manifestation of Union sentiment in this region occurred in November, 1861. William Blount Carter of Elizabethton, Tennessee, conceived a plan of burning all the river bridges of the section simultaneously, thus making it easier for the Federal troops to advance and take over. He submitted the plan to the North, and it was personally and enthusiastically approved by President Lincoln after Secretary Seward and General McClellan had passed on it. Specifically, the plan called for burning on the same night the nine river bridges between Bristol, Tennessee-Virginia, and Stevenson, Alabama. By doing this, a stretch of two hundred twenty-five miles of railroad would be made useless, and the military communications between Virginia and this part of Tennessee would be seriously impaired. The plan was put into effect. Carter had carefully selected a half-dozen Unionists who lived in the vicinity of each bridge. In the dead of night, at the appointed hour, these arsonists struck and in five instances were successful. In the others, Confederate guns and knives prevailed. Six of the Unionists were captured and five of them were hanged by order of Judah P. Benjamin, Confederate Secretary of War. The sixth was a man named Harrison Self, who was imprisoned at Knoxville awaiting execution. It happened that he was so well esteemed among his neighbors that several high-ranking Confederate officers petitioned the Richmond authorities to save his life, but to no avail. Then Self's beautiful daughter, who learned only on the morning of the execution day that her father was to be put to death, became so heartbroken and wept so sorrowfully that she finally persuaded the crusty Parson Brownlow, who was in the same jail at the time, to write out the following telegram for her:

Knoxville, December 26, 1861

HON. JEFFERSON DAVIS:

My father, Harrison Self, is sentenced to hang at four o'clock this evening on a charge of bridge burning. As he remains my earthly all, and all my hopes of happiness center upon him, I implore you to pardon him.

Elizabeth Self

President Davis responded with a pardon, and her father was saved.

The burning of the bridges served to show how intense was the Union sentiment in East Tennessee, and caused the Confederate leaders to station stronger guards in its mountains and valleys. Even so, an audacious convention of Union men was held at Greeneville, the home of Andrew Johnson, at which resolutions were passed condemning the state for leaving the Union, and affirming the right of every man to work out his own destiny as far as the war was concerned. Oliver P. Temple, one of the leaders present, wrote afterward that this convention was one of the most notable meetings ever held in the United States. It was conducted almost in the face of the Confederate Army which controlled the region. "Only a few miles away," wrote Temple, "the Great Smoky Mountains rose up and stretched away in matchless grandeur and sublimity, immovable and unchangeable, typical of the steadfastness of the brave people who dwelt in the valleys spreading out from their base."

One hero emerged from the bridge-burning episode. He was James Keelin, the Confederate guard stationed at Strawberry Plains, near Knoxville. Keelin was a member of the Thomas Legion, a regiment consisting almost entirely of Cherokee Indians who were fighting the North. Forty Federals attacked him in the night, but he resolutely stood his ground and savagely fought back. He was shot in the side, in the left hand, and in the hip. Again and again the Federals charged him, but in some miraculous manner he made them retire. Finally his left hand was cut off, his right hand split, and he was severely wounded by saber cuts on his head and body. But he stood firm. At last the Federals, believing that the stand of the unflinching Keelin surely indicated that reinforcements were near at hand, withdrew. They counted three of their number dead and several others wounded. Keelin was laid up for twelve months. Just as soon as he recovered, he rejoined the Confederate Army. Asked by an officer how he had managed to handle the attacking Federal troops, he replied:

"By God sir, I surrounded 'em!"

The recruiting, like the discipline of the Southern soldiers, oftentimes left something to be desired, according to a report of a noncombatant, W. B. Lenoir of Sweetwater. He told of one Confederate soldier named Carter who "joined up because some secession ladies of Hiwassee community made a flag, cooked a big dinner, held a big rally and got a politician to speak along these lines: The Yankees want to take our property, free our Negroes, violate states' rights and force us into submission." Whereupon the ardent hostesses waved the Stars and Bars, a fifer struck up *Dixie,* and a drummer rattled the snare drum. "Fall in, boys!" exhorted the eloquent speaker. "We won't be gone more than three or four months and we'll come back covered with glory. Whoopee! Hurrah!" Carter had no property and had never seen more than half a dozen Negroes in his life. He knew nothing about states' rights. But having worked as a tenant most of his life, he thought it would be great to ride a horse, wear a uniform, lie around the campfire, and swap yarns with the boys. Just a big picnic, he thought. So he joined up . . . only to find out soon the dismal truth about long and bloody war. There were others, however, not so gullible. The landowners, many of them well heeled, hired others to go in their places, paying as high as a thousand dollars per substitute. Still others did not wish to be bothered with either war or substitutes, so hid out in the woods and lived nomadic lives until the great contest was over.

One of the most colorful soldiers of the campaigns in this region was Brigadier General John H. Morgan, a Confederate cavalry commander some of whose exploits rank with those of the famous Nathan Bedford Forrest. Loved by his men and renowned for his daring, Morgan carried out several important raids in East Tennessee and Kentucky, once leading his men as far as Ohio, where he was captured and imprisoned, only to dig a tunnel under the jail, escape, and return South. He had an effective way of falling quickly upon the enemy with his fast horsemen, fighting with great fury, then suddenly dividing his forces and making his getaway before the surprised Federals could recover. Though at no time did his force number more than four thousand, his raiders are said to have killed and wounded that many of the enemy, and captured over fifteen thousand of them. A handsome man from a good family, he not only was adored by his men but was looked upon with great favor by the women. His irregular capture of enemy property, and the robbing of a bank in his territory, won him comparison, up North, with the Missouri bandit Quantrill, but all Southern sources deny the justice of this. Some Yankee newspapers referred to him as "a horse thief." Opie Read wrote of the time when, as a young boy, he persuaded a half-drunken bugler of Morgan's men to let him ride with them on one of the raids in Tennessee. It was early morning and the dashing Confederate force of cavalry rode jauntily forth through the beautiful countryside, singing as they galloped along to the accompaniment of the awakened birds. Heavy dew sparkled on the grass as the sun glinted from it, then from the resting bayonets of the sleeping Federal force. As the Northern men awoke, Morgan's unsteady bugler, with whom Read was riding, sounded a charge and the swift raiders swooped into the Federal lines like so many deadly birds. The Yankees scrambled sleepily to their feet and tried to return the fire. Again the bugler lifted his horn to his lips, but this time there was no sound. He fell against young Read. He was dead.

The death of General Morgan himself has always been a strange and sad episode in the history of this region, so different was it from the fate of other daring leaders. The war was nearing its end, his force had been considerably reduced, and Morgan himself seemed to have lost some of that intrepid spirit which led his men to so many picturesque victories. It was September 4, 1864, and he and his men had arrived at Greeneville, where he was to spend the night prior to making an attack on the Federals next day. As was the custom for generals on both sides, he stayed at the home of Mrs. Catharine Williams, who owned the biggest house in town. Mrs. Williams had two sons; and, following the familiar pattern of the region, one was in the Confederate, one in the Union Army. The wife of the Union son was at that time staying with Mrs. Williams, and was known as a strong sympathizer with the North; in fact, it was later reported that she had informed the Federals Morgan was there. It rained hard that night, and as Morgan sat with his staff in the parlor of the Williams home, the singing of the younger men was almost drowned out by the noise of the thunder and rain. The general sat in a corner of the room, a serious look on his face as he whistled a melancholy tune. He did not talk much, but once called a staff officer over and told him that the Federals had stated they would never take him alive. After making sure that his pickets were properly placed around the town, Morgan went to bed. Toward morning, he and his staff were awakened by the sound of rifle shots. They quickly arose, only to find that a Union force of considerable size had surrounded the house. The Confederates stole into the back yard and made a dash to escape, but Morgan was seen by a mounted Federal trooper in the street, who cursed the general and shot him. He fell face-downward, dying on the wet leaves and grass of the yard. Years later, Basil Duke, who was his second-in-command and succeeded him, wrote: "Surely men never grieved for a leader as Morgan's men sorrowed for him."

It is not the intention here to discuss the general progress of the war in the Smoky Mountain Country. Some of its crucial battles were fought at Knoxville and around Chattanooga. Here was the center of fratricidal strife — one extreme example being Champe Ferguson, an uneducated mountaineer who was not only a Confederate guide in Tennessee but a notoriously fierce and cunning character besides. The episode is mentioned in the books of John Fox, Jr. Ferguson had a brother in the Union Army, and throughout the long war the two sought each other with cruel persistence. In 1865 Champe was captured and executed. Just before being put to death, he delivered a stirring speech about his past, ascribing his ferocious hatred of his brother and antagonism toward the North to a mad desire for revenge for the death of his child, whom he claimed the Yankees had killed.

Countless small skirmishes were fought in Tennessee and North Carolina. Union men and their families were never safe from their Confederate neighbors, and vice-versa. Many persons found the mountains a perfect place for hiding. Guerrilla warfare raged almost continuously, and continued even after Lee's surrender at Appomattox. Near Soddy in East Tennessee there occurred a fantastic incident known locally as Clift's War. A well-to-do Unionist named William Clift who lived there got into the habit of shielding Union sympathizers on their way to Kentucky to join the Federal Army. His "business" became so extensive that he began to use an empty Cumberland Presbyterian encampment on the banks of a nearby creek. It was not long before the camp was so full of refugees that it resembled a military post. Confederate leaders got word of the encampment, and from the exaggerated reports felt that it was a real military threat. They resolved to capture it. About two thousand men from Cleveland and from Bradley County formed the expedition. Part of this Southern force advanced from one side, part from another. Inside the encampment, "Colonel" Clift didn't possess so much as a popgun in the way of arms. But he did rig up a big iron pipe to resemble a cannon, mounted it with its end toward the invaders, and under cover of night slipped away with his Unionists, unseen by the Confederates. The latter prepared for battle. They sent scouts, reconnoitered, dispatched patrols, and generally deployed for a long siege against the "heavy artillery" the scouts had reported. In their advance, one Southern force got mixed up and fired on a body of its own men, which immediately retreated, and much excitement and some shooting ensued before it was discovered that there was not a man or a gun inside and that the "fort" was a deserted church camp.

After Tennessee was taken by the Northern forces, it was not long before the choleric Parson Brownlow returned to Knoxville and to the editorship of his newspaper. In his first postexilic editorial he showed again his vengeful spirit. Wrote he: "We endorse all Lincoln has done and find fault with him for not having done more. The Federal government has been too lenient. . . . The mediation we shall advocate is that of the cannon and the sword." As if this ominous promise was to be made official, Brownlow soon became governor of the state. Fortunately, there were cooler heads, such as Andrew Johnson and his supporters, who took a merciful view toward the South. But this part of the country was to bear its heavy cross for many more years to come. As the radicals gained possession of the national Congress, so did they control on a smaller scale the state governments of the South. But what they had to govern was mainly remnants.

The beauteous Tennessee Valley at the foot of the Smokies was a dreary, blasted wasteland. The fences had been burned, the apple, pear, and plum trees cut down. Along the roads stood the ashen walls of once-magnificent mansions which had graced a countryside enlivened by their occupants, many of whom were to see the fair land no more, some dead at the hands of kinsmen. No other part of the South had endured continuous warfare on such a scale as East Tennessee, and it looked like Georgia after Sherman's infamous March to the Sea. Public buildings had been destroyed, real estate had dropped in value by one-half. But the greatest damage, of course, was human. There was longing for those who did not return; but for those who did, there was usually nothing left but empty poverty, domestic struggles, and even murder. Brothers who once loved each other were forever estranged. Neighbors who had lived in peaceful happiness now, because of sectional differences, were at each other's throats. A great, collective family had been split asunder.

Dry Wind of Reconstruction

When the dry wind of reconstruction swept across the mountains, it seemed at first to be the breath of further destruction. The Confederates had raided their Union neighbors. Now it was the Unionists' turn. But to the great chagrin of local Northern sympathizers, the occupying Federal troops did not discriminate between those who had been on one side and those on the other. To them, all were Rebels and were to be subordinated, punished, and crushed. When property was wanted, it was taken, no matter whose it was. When the carpetbagging soldiers hurled insults, they were given broadside to all present. So it was that in the end virtually all the people of the South grew to resent and dread the heavy hand of the victorious Federal government, which had once promised amnesty but had largely forgotten it.

Confederates under bond to appear before the Federal court in Knoxville were afraid to be seen in the area because of the violence meted out by bandits and self-styled avengers. The Unionists demanded that the ex-Rebels leave that part of the state, and most of them did. Blanket warnings were posted. One of these, given below, shows the caliber of many of those who issued the threats:

SPECIAL ORDER NO 1
In the woods near Newmarket, Tenn.
July 24, 1865

All damed rebels are hereby notified at lieve at wonce, if found her at the expiration of ten days from the date of this order and no preparation to lieve Thrashing machines will sit at wonce enough to thrash all crops with the usual tole hickry withs and cowhides or anything else that may be required on the occasion. We are working by the order that you theving God forsaken helldeserving Rebels issued four years ago that Union men and Rebels cannot live together which we find now not altogether bogus.

> *We are vary*
> *respectively*
> *Old Soldier*

Even war can bring some benefits, however, and the land of the Smoky Mountains was no exception. Many of the young men who had joined the Union or Confederate armies had previously not been more than a few miles from home. In the course of their war travels they saw new states, new ways of farming, new methods of doing business, new ways to dress and have fun, and improved systems of education. The army into which many of them had gone as a frolic taught them mass discipline, the rewards of ability and hard work and how to get along with other men of different personalities and viewpoints. Those who went North learned that heavy industry was a great economic factor in our nation, in fact, the one which weighted the war in favor of the Yankee. There was much money in the North, it was found. Some of the Southerners, realizing that their Confederate money was now worthless, persuaded their newly made Northern friends to become interested in the South as a good place for investment; and the results of this may still be seen in the resurrected Southern economy. In the Smoky Mountains, the wild game that had gone virtually unmolested for four years while the hunters were out after human targets, had increased manyfold and proved a great boon of food in the lean years which followed.

In 1866 the State of Tennessee, which was the last to leave the Union, became the first to return to it. Following the administration of the radical Brownlow, the fortunes of the state began to take an upswing. The Negroes, who for a time had thought that their freedom also meant freedom from work, learned better, won the right to vote, got better schools, and generally came to be assimilated more into everyday life. They had never been a big problem in East Tennessee, and were not a problem now. The ex-soldiers of the Union and the Confederacy grew to forget their main differences, and learned to live side by side again as citizens of one nation. The soldier had had his day in the field. Now it was time to make good at home.

IV

The War of the Roses

THE most idyllic and colorful example of folksy American politics in our nation's history was Tennessee's War of the Roses. It is still fondly recalled by its contemporaries, and almost as strongly revered by the state's younger generation.

"Take Alf and me, for instance," said Robert L. Taylor. "Born of the same mother and nursed at the same breasts — but Alf's milk soured on him and he became a Republican!"

So remarked one of Tennessee's gubernatorial candidates in the race of 1886, speaking from the same platform as his opponent and brother, Alfred A. Taylor.

The "War of the Roses," as some one had dubbed it in commemoration of ancestral England, was brother against brother. Only one third of a century before, brother had opposed brother in this same region, but that conflict was physical and bloody. Now it was verbal, clean, and sportsmanlike. Even the speeches were flowery. It was a forty-five-year carryover from the days of "Tippecanoe and Tyler Too," when William Henry Harrison and John Tyler rode into the presidential office on the crest of a log-cabin-and-hard-cider wave of popular enthusiasm — another reiteration of the homely truth that Americans like color in their politics.

The War of the Roses contrasted with the Civil War and the conflict of loyalty between East Tennessee and the rest of the State. In the battles which rocked the valleys and reverberated against the eastern mountains where the young Taylor brothers were just growing up, kinsmen fought and killed one another, and other wounds were inflicted — wounds to the intimacy and affection of relatives and neighbors — which the end of the war did not heal. In the dim half-light of the Reconstruction period in Tennessee, those who sat scornfully in the seats of the rulers were not Northern carpetbaggers, as was the usual post-bellum custom, but native Tennesseans, mostly from the eastern part, who had been on the winning side. This situation made the problems of Reconstruction all the more acute.

Nor did peace return to this section with the exit of the Reconstruction radicals in 1870. Tennessee had by then acquired a heavy public debt, and interest rates were piling it depressingly high. Legislators and most of the people were inclined to regard it as a war debt, foisted upon them by the Reconstructionists, and felt no real responsibility for paying it off. The working classes didn't care a whoop whether the bonds were ever redeemed or not, if such redemption meant raising taxes. With the economic situation what it was, the people had no money for taxes anyway. Added to this problem were those of regulation of the railroads, prison reform, liquor control, and inadequate local education. As a result, the public was in a grim state of mind, and the War of the Roses came as a welcome diversion from care and uncertainty. The merry campaign of Bob and Alf Taylor held music and laughter as refreshing as a mountain breeze.

The first of their forty-one joint debates was opened at Madisonville, a little county-seat town in the shadow of the Great Smokies. It is the home town of United States Senator Estes Kefauver and has always been a hotbed of local politics. The campaign was to catapult the Taylor brothers into state and national prominence, and make them forever a part of the best traditions of the Volunteer State. The now almost legendary contest would take its place with the other mellow souvenirs of the upland country, with fiddle music, the Bible, and good eating-tobacco; for years the huddles in country stores would talk of it; and today, among the old-timers of the region, it calls glowingly back those golden days "when things was lots better 'n they are now."

The campaign ground was largely rural, and the isolated farmers, who had few diversions, regarded public speaking as a favorite type of entertainment. On Saturdays they came into the county seats on foot or horseback to listen to the court trials, between which they congregated in the court-yards, chewed tobacco, and swapped yarns and horses. Ministers, following the lead of the late Samuel Doak, customarily preached sermons a half-day in length, closed out by hour-long prayers and then the very necessary Sunday dinner on the ground.

Bob and Alf Taylor were appropriately born in Happy Valley in upper East Tennessee, the sons of Nathaniel G. Taylor, a lawyer-preacher-politician and Whig congressman from the state's traditionally Republican First District. But his wife, their mother, was the sister of Landon C. Haynes, Confederate senator from Tennessee. This was the basis for

Alf's being a Republican and his brother Bob, a strong admirer of Senator Haynes, a Democrat.

How evenly divided politically were the Taylor forebears is illustrated by the following story about David Haynes, maternal grandfather of the candidates. One day during the Civil War, a troop of Confederate cavalry which was operating in East Tennessee came upon Mr. Haynes near his home. Their leader asked who he was. "Sir," replied Haynes, "I have the honor to be the father of Confederate Senator Landon C. Haynes." With salutes and cheers, the soldiers rode on. Soon there came a detachment of Union cavalry following in hot pursuit. To a similar inquiry by them, Haynes said. "I am the father of a daughter who, gentlemen, had the good sense to accept the matrimonial offer of the Honorable Nathaniel G. Taylor, late of Congress and now supporting President Lincoln and the Union." The soldiers cheered and rode away.

Soon after finishing college at Athens, Tennessee, Alf and Bob entered politics and remained in it the rest of their eventful lives. Both of them had a talent for dramatics, story-telling, and rare good humor. Their early days on the farm in beautiful Happy Valley had been a fine period of training in debate. Almost daily in the fields where they were at work, the brothers argued some public question. Alf would mount a stump, lumber pile, or feedbox, whichever happened to be handy, and deliver a speech from the Republican viewpoint on some national issue. Bob would follow with the Democratic answer. Audiences were never lacking. The farmhands and neighbors would drop everything and listen to the youthful orators match wits, encouraging them with hearty applause and cheers. The only drawback to this pastime was the time and money wasted by the enthusiastic performers and their rapt listeners; and their father finally put a stop to the debates, but not before Alf and Bob had gained valuable experience in real "stump speaking." Only once did they lose their tempers. One called the other a liar, and they were about to come to blows when suddenly their mother appeared and gave them both such an eloquent tonguelashing that the boys never forgot it.

In their school days the Taylor brothers wrote, directed, produced, and starred in a comedy entitled *Horatio Spriggins of the Firm of Muggins, Spriggins and Scruggins.* A sample from this hilariously received play, which raised enough money to carpet a lot of Methodist churches in the region, was given the writer by Colonel Milton Ochs of the Chattanooga *Times,* a contemporary of the Taylors'.

A mountaineer is on the witness stand in a murder trial.

"Tell the jury what you know about the murder on Hell Creek," says the district attorney.

"I don't know much about it," replies the witness.

"Then tell what you know."

"All I know is this," drawls the witness. "We was all up thar at the big dance celebratin' Robert E. Lee's birthday. The fiddles was playin' and we was swingin' corners, and the boys got to slappin' each other on the back as they swung. Finally one of them slapped too hard and the other knocked him down. His brother shot that feller, and that feller's brother cut t'other feller's throat, and the feller that was knocked down drawed his knife and cut that feller's liver out; the old man of the house got mad and run to the bed, turned up the tick and grabbed his shotgun and turned both barrels loose on the crowd, and I saw there was goin' to be trouble and I left."

Ironically, it was a split in the Republican ranks in East

Tennessee, a not-uncommon occurrence, that gave Bob Taylor his headstart over Alf, an advantage he was always to exploit. The trouble occurred in 1878 and was a reaction to the excessive Unionism of Tennessee's Andrew Johnson, who had died three years before. Most of the small farmers of the state were Democrats and had been since the time of Andrew Jackson, who had solidified this agrarian element behind him when he went from Tennessee to the White House as the fiery, popular advocate of the common man. The same rural element was nurtured by Polk, and later was successfully wooed by Andrew Johnson, who entered the White House as a Union Republican. It was the loss of this support which divided the party, and as a result of the split Republican Alf Taylor was finally knocked out of the race.

Bob was nominated for Congress by the Democrats, and although only twenty-eight at the time, his aptness at telling anecdotes and acting out his speeches had immediate success. In the campaign he was running against the veteran Republican, Major A. H. Pettibone. The latter, in a speech, ridiculed Bob for his use of the fiddle in their debates. After Pettibone had finished and sat down, Bob arose, placed his fiddle upon the speaker's table, and laid beside it a carpetbag. He then turned to his audience and asked them to choose between the two. They did. Bob was soon in Congress. In his try for reelection, however, he was defeated; but he had become politically known.

In the gubernatorial campaign of 1886, the state Democrats faced a crisis. Their internal factions — the Bourbons, led by that extreme advocate of states' rights, Governor Isham G. Harris, and the more liberal element of the party, the Mugwumps — were fighting each other over the state debt and the supervision of railroads; and their strife threatened to wreck the party. So both groups welcomed Bob Taylor with his fiddle and jokes. His task was one of conciliation, and he was perfectly qualified for the job. His speeches were not models of logic or political brilliance, but they were hilariously entertaining, which was more important at the time. Bob's political value lay in his immense popularity with the ordinary people, his independence of party leaders, and his natural ability as a peacemaker. He had never belonged to any party group, so there was no extreme opposition to him by any. His father and grandfathers were moderates, and Bob's own non-participation in the Civil War — he was too young — gave him an unusual appeal for the young men of the state and did not arouse the bitter feelings too often rampant in the "bloody shirt" era. He chose to forget the animosity of the War between the States, and his wide personal popularity enabled him to ignore the prejudiced factions. His was an era when the generals, colonels, and "majuhs" were just beginning to relinquish their hold upon the politics of Tennessee and other Southern states. Both Bob and Alf felt that it was high time to wrest the government from the scourge of the "brigadiers," who still chose to contest in their minds the decision which had been rendered at Appomattox. Bob's nomination in 1886 was therefore a victory for progressive forces more important than any race for governor.

Bob did not take an active part in his nomination. He sent word to the convention that he would not accept it unless he was chosen by all factions of the party. A prime reason why he did not play an active role was because he had been appointed United States pension agent at Knoxville, and the law forbade his active participation in political campaigns.

Prior to this appointment, he had run a weekly newspaper, the *Comet,* in Johnson City, and had lost so much money that the paper sometimes had to skip publication for lack of funds. So his well-paying federal appointment came in handy. It had been slow in coming, though. After waiting many weeks, Bob had sent a typical telegram:

GROVER CLEVELAND
PRESIDENT, U.S.
WASHINGTON, D.C.

That other fellow is still drawing my pay.

Robt. L. Taylor

The appointment came through the next day.

After being nominated, Bob received a telegram from the committee asking if he would accept. He wired back.

DEMOCRATIC NOMINATING COMMITTEE
NASHVILLE, TENNESSEE

A seedy individual whom we once knew appeared at my mother's home and said "Emerline, effen you don't believe I can carry a ham home, just try me."

Robt. L. Taylor

The Republicans nominated Alf Taylor, and that's about all there was to it. The selection was without incident and had much less political significance. There were now no factions among the Republicans; they were a strong and united minority party. Alf had only one opponent and was chosen on the first ballot. The dissenters within the Democratic ranks laughed and said this ruined any chances of Bob's winning because of the grotesque, irreverent situation of a brother running against his own brother. One editor suggested that the Taylor family hold a caucus to select the next governor of Tennessee. Actually, how close the contest came to being a three-cornered one is shown by the fact that the father of the Taylor brothers, former Congressman Nathaniel G. Taylor, was urged by the Prohibition Party to accept its nomination and run in the same race. He wisely refused, thus avoiding a farce; and added this unfavorable comment: "I think it is a shame for my boys to run against each other." He refused to vote. Mrs. Taylor was afraid the campaign would cause her sons to hate each other, but its first debate allayed these fears. Said Bob:

"I have a very high regard for the Republican candidate — he is a perfect gentleman, because he is my brother. I have asked him to come with me and I would furnish him with crowds and introduce him in society. We are two roses from the same garden."

Whereupon the appellation "War of the Roses" was applied, and Bob donned a white rose, Alf a red one.

There was no political collusion. Although each brother respected and liked the other and neither lost his temper even in their hottest wrangles, it was a serious contest from a party standpoint. Each aimed to show up to the better political advantage.

Their routine ran something like this: rival delegations met each of the candidates at the depot of the particular town where they were to speak, and in fringed surries drawn by smartly harnessed horses led a procession to the hotel where the candidate was to stay. This was always the same hotel for both men, since they not only stayed at the same place but in the same room and slept in the same bed at night. One reason for this arrangement was the necessity for keeping expenses down to a minimum. Unlike today, when candidates enjoy lavish campaign funds, the Taylors depended mainly on their means and the bare essentials furnished by personal friends who were active in the campaign.

The carriage of Alf was invariably adorned with red roses and red streamers, and drawn by eight roan horses topped with red plumes. The other carriages, surries, and buggies which followed, as well as the horsemen, were decorated with red pennants, ribbons, bunting, and confetti along with the inevitable bountiful bunches of rich red roses. This "long red line" would extend a mile or two depending on the size of the town. Bob's procession was the same, except that the motif was white. No knightly pageant or modern festival ever outshone these parades in pomp and floral splendor. The audiences were never less than six thousand in number; in Nashville the gathering was estimated at twenty-five thousand, a good number even for today. At each stop of consequence a featured event was the presentation, by the most beautiful lady in the community, of red and white bouquets made into the shapes of horseshoes, harps, and fiddles.

At the hotel an initial speech was made, a lot of hands were shaken; then in a few hours a formal debate took place in the main part of town. This procedure was repeated in the evening, except that the theme was more social, flowers and gifts again being forthcoming from the ladies, bless them! After the business part of the meeting was over and Bob and Alf had given their all for their parties, the climax came. Both brothers played the fiddle. In this important accomplishment Alf was better than Bob, but the latter made up for any lack of musicianship by more conspicuous gestures and motions, shaking and wiggling from head to foot in the most exaggerated and comical manner. The festival would go on until midnight, to the great joy of the crowds. Next morning early, the Taylor brothers could be seen driving away together in a rented hack to some small outlying hamlet, talking and joshing with each other and comparing notes on their experiences of the previous day.

Their schedule was worked out jointly by the Democratic and Republican state committees, and it went on like this for a full three months. Alf was serious; he talked in a somewhat bumbling Hamiltonian manner but with undisputed sincerity. The younger Bob, on the other hand, was a born clown, tall, easy of manner, and fluent; and when he told the funny stories of which he was a master, he would assume a look of serious drollery that made the humor sidesplitting. On the rare occasions when Alf told a joke he would laugh heartily with the crowds. The candidates inherited some of their style. Both Landon C. Haynes and Nathaniel G. Taylor had been eminent orators in the period from 1850 to 1860, "with a facility for a certain kind of word painting and for rhetorical effects."

Not all listeners liked the verbal style of the War of the Roses, however. One editor referred to Bob's oratory as "wheyish slop" and got tired of the "daily slush, even to nausea." Bob was termed by another writer a "fiddler, statesman and buffoon." These, though, were exceptional sentiments, for most newspapers caught the spirit of the amiable occasion and spurred the contestants on with witticisms of their own. It was a field day for the jesters, an interlude of comic relief in a time of anxiety.

When the brother-candidates reached Chattanooga, that city treated their arrival as a very special occasion. Elaborate plans had been made for the reception, and the respective committees had jointly provided a program for the day. The climax was to be a serenade at night, followed by speeches from the balcony of the hotel. Both candidates had agreed to prepare a special address for the occasion. First was to come incidental music to Bob, then his peroration, followed by the same routine for Alf. During the afternoon of the great day, Alf was sitting at a table in his room, revising his speech, when his committee called him into another room. Leaving the manuscript on the table, he went to the meeting, which proved to be an important one lasting until evening. In fact, while it was still going on brass bands appeared under the window and launched into *Dixie*. Then the music stopped, and the voice of the master of ceremonies was heard introducing Bob Taylor. Alf had been paying little attention to the outside sounds, knowing he did not appear on the program until later, but suddenly he sat bolt-upright, as the voice of his brother pealed out, speaking strangely familiar words:

"The illustrious dreamers and creators in the realm of music have scaled the purple steeps of the heaven of sweet sounds, unbarred its opal gates and opened the holy of holies . . ."

"Good heavens!" cried Alf. "That's my speech!"

Rushing back into his room, he found his manuscript gone.

As soon as Bob had finished delivering Alf's speech, he and his committee dashed back into the room shaking with laughter. Now it was Alf's turn — and he had to face the great throng totally unprepared. He stuttered and sweated through an impromptu effort, and swore he would get even.

Alf had not long to wait. Soon after reaching Fayetteville, both candidates as usual went to their room, and Bob left almost immediately to call on some of the political leaders of the town. Alf seized the opportunity for a nap, but had no more than lain down when a loud knocking sounded on the door. He opened it to find a "passel" of Democrats who had ridden into town on horseback to greet their Bob. Never having seen the Taylors before, and having been told this was Bob's room, they took it for granted that Alf was their man, and before he could explain they were slapping him on the back and otherwise extending hearty greetings. Then one of the party announced that they had ridden twenty miles that day and were hot and dry.

"We need jist a leetle nip to straighten us up," he added. Bob was known to have liberal views on liquor, while Alf was dry. Drawing back in indignation, the latter said sternly:

"Gentlemen, I cannot conceive of how you can make such a request! I would have you understand that I am a temperance man from the crown of my head to the soles of my feet. Oh God, that men should put an enemy in their mouth to steal away their brains. Why before I would be instrumental in polluting your lips with one single drop of the hellish stuff, I would surrender my nomination, give up the race, and allow Alf Taylor to be elected governor!"

Bob's supporters quickly dispersed.

The brothers would play jokes on each other, but they were never seriously antagonistic. Bob's grandson, the well-known Memphis attorney Robert L. Taylor, told this writer that at one stop the audience heckled Alf because he was a Republican, whereupon Bob got up and announced that if they didn't stop it, *he* would walk off the platform and not speak.

The campaign was colorful and its effects were lasting. It was a forerunner of the hillbilly-band type of race which is still popular in the South and West, as evidenced by the number of governors and senators who in recent years have gone into office on the wings of fiddle music and clowning.

The 1948 senatorial campaign of Congressman B. Carroll Reece, former Republican national chairman, incorporated a good many of the Taylor brothers' techniques.

It was the day of spread-eagle oratory, of fine forensic flourishes, and the speaker who could paint the most elaborately beautiful word pictures and wring the most tears or coax the most laughter was the winner. Bob Taylor filled his speeches with touching descriptions of the Great Beyond, and turned loose amazing euphuisms; Alf was not far behind, but his was the more formal delivery. Bob would alternately bathe his audience in tears, then shake them with laughter, ranging from the glory of Almighty God to a sprightly fiddle version of *Old Dan Tucker*. A favorite device was to pretend he had had a magnificent dream, then bring his audience into it with him. Inevitably there was the humor. For example, he told of the oldtime Negro minister who was closing his sermon while Uncle Rastus, who had been playing cards until late the night before, sat over in the amen corner sound asleep. Announced the preacher: "We will now close this here meetin' with prayer, and we will ask Brother Rastus to lead."

Suddenly aroused from his slumber, Rastus shouted. "It ain't my lead. I jist dealt!"

Bob never missed a bet. On another occasion he said: "It ought to be the universal law that none but fat men and bald-headed men should be the heads of families, because they are always so good-natured, contented and easily managed. There is more music in a fat man's laugh than there is in a thousand orchestras. Fat sides and bald heads are the symbols of music, innocence and meek submission. Oh ladies, listen to the words of wisdom. Cultivate the society of fat men, for of such is the kingdom of heaven. And the fat women — God bless their sober sides — they are things of beauty and a joy forever."

As far as state issues were concerned, there were no serious ones between the opposing candidates. Bob and Alf differed more on national problems. The Republicans at that time were demanding repeal of the internal revenue system, labeling it as inefficient; but the biggest controversy revolved around the questions of the tariff and the Blair education bill, and these two issues were the basic points of difference between the platforms of Bob and Alf Taylor. The national Democratic Party under Grover Cleveland had straddled the question of the tariff because the party was divided on it. The Republicans, of course, stood for a high tariff. The Blair bill, sponsored by Senator Blair of New Hampshire, proposed — even in those days! — federal aid to education, especially in the South. Actually it was cleverly designed to get rid of a surplus of money piled up in the Treasury; and by giving this lagniappe to the South, the Republicans thought that it would in return be more sympathetic to their high tariff views. The states'-righters, toward whom Bob Taylor inclined, took the view that such assistance would result in federal domination of the local schools.

But tariff, internal revenue, or education did not dominate the War of the Roses. Bob could not stay dull. When he wasn't cracking jokes, he was making them. Between two major stops the Taylors, tired from a long day of buggy travel, stopped at a farmhouse to spend the night. The host was a lifelong Republican and a devoted follower of Alf. As usual the brothers slept in the same bed. Next morning at four o'clock the enterprising Bob arose, dressed without waking Alf, and went downstairs. In the gray pre-dawn light he made his way to the woodpile, cut a lot of stovewood, carried it in, and built a fire in the kitchen stove. Then he went to the spring and toted a couple of buckets of water to the house. By now the man of the house was awake and up. Seeing a fire in the stove, he went to the barn to feed the livestock. There he found the horses already fed their corn, and Bob up in the loft pitching down their hay with a fork. Going back to the house, the Democratic candidate obtained a bucket and proceeded to milk the cows while his host fed the hogs. It was now time for breakfast, and Alf was still snoring away upstairs. In fact, the host had to go up and shake him before he would get up. The farmer came back downstairs, and while they waited on Alf he called Bob aside and said.

"Son, I've voted the Republican ticket all my life and I never intended to scratch it, but I'll be goldarned if I don't do it this time for you. Anybody that is as lazy as that Alf ain't fit to be governor of this here state."

What was probably Bob Taylor's most famous story, which later became a feature of the lecture tours he and Alf made across the country following their political campaigns, concerned a new preacher in a Smoky Mountain community, one Brother Billy Patterson, and the town bully, Bert Lynch. In the preacher's first sermon he roundly condemned the devil, sin, and all kinds of evil including whiskey; but especially did he condemn Bert Lynch as a moral coward and a brute. This infuriated the bully, and he determined to give Brother Patterson a sound thrashing the next time they met. In a few days they came face to face on a mountain trail.

"Parson," said Bert grimly, "you had yore turn last Sunday; it's mine today. Pull off that broadcloth and take yore medicine; I'm a'gwine to suck the marrow out'n them old bones o' yourn."

The preacher pleaded with the bully, but to no avail. Finally he said: "Well, if nothing but a fight will do you, will you let me kneel down and say my prayer before we fight?"

"All right," said Bert, "but make it short."

The preacher kneeled down, and prayed thus:

"O Lord, Thou knowest when I killed Bill Cummings and John Brown and Jerry Smith and Levi Bottles, that I did it in self-defense. Thou knowest, O Lord, that when I cut the heart out of young Slinger and strewed the ground with the brains of Paddy Miles, that it was forced upon me and that I did it in great agony of soul. And now, O Lord, I am about to be forced to put in his coffin this poor, miserable wretch who has attacked me here today. O Lord, have mercy upon his soul and take care of his helpless widow and orphans when he is gone."

Whereupon he arose, whetting the blade of his knife on the sole of his shoe, and singing:

"Hark! from the tombs a doleful sound,

"Mine ears attend the cry."

But when he looked around, Bert was gone. There was nothing in sight but a little cloud of dust far up the road.

The War of the Roses ended in the mountain region where it began, at Blountville in the upper Smokies. The Taylor brothers had spoken, fiddled, and joked before a million people, a real achievement in those days. Bob had opened the campaign. Now Alf closed it. Said he:

"My countrymen, a few words and I will end my connection with the most remarkable contest which our country has witnessed. . . . We have striven, my brother and I, with all our might in the defense of the principles which each believed to be right. . . . I say to you now that after all these eventful struggles, I still love my brother, love him as of old with undying affection — but politically, my friends, I despise him."

The voters decided — to the tune of a thirteen-thousand majority for Bob, an unprecedented Democratic lead. However, Alf set a record too, receiving the largest Republican vote up to that time.

But the picturesque and exciting contest was only the beginning of the Taylor brothers' careers. Bob went on to attain the distinction of being governor for three terms, congressman once, and senator. Alf was elected governor too — but not until after Bob had been laid to rest eight years. Alf was also elected to Congress for three terms from the First Congressional District, the third member of his family to reach this position, his father and Bob having gotten there previously — the only instance, it is believed, in which a father and his two sons have represented the same constituency in Congress.

On July 30, 1950, Governor Gordon Browning of Tennessee made a speech in Happy Valley, home place of the Taylors, on the one hundredth anniversary of the birth of Bob. Speaking of the days when, as a young man, he knew Bob and watched him in oratorical action, the governor said:

"There was kindled in my heart an overweening passion to emulate his experience."

How well Browning grew to emulate his ideal may be determined by comparing the ending of his address that day with the following quotation which he gave from a speech of Bob Taylor:

"What Heaven is, I know not, but I long have dreamed of its purple hills and its fields of light, blossoming with immortal beauty; of its brooks of laughter and its rivers of song and its palace of eternal love. . . . But what care I for crown of stars and harp of gold, if I can love and laugh and sing with my loved ones forever in the smile of my Savior and my God."

Governor Browning closed his tribute with these words:

"If we would truly honor his memory this day, in fancy we must hear his voice calling across to us from the other bank of eternity, saying to the people of Tennessee that, so long as her mountain barriers stand, so long as her rivers roll on to the sea, so long as the blessed sunlight of God's heaven delights her pulsing heart, may no citizen corrupt the fair expression of the people's will."

V

Folkways in a Static Society

In the Smoky Mountain Country around the turn of the century, time stood still. It was a static society and a happy one. The only regular visitor to the back regions was the sun, and even it did not penetrate into some of the deepest coves. The winding and narrow mountain roads made it hard to get in and out. Being virtually self-sufficient anyway, raising or making all that they ordinarily needed, the rural folks had little necessity or desire to get out. Why bother about the rest of the world when one could live happy here?

The effects of the Civil War between the States had just about faded into the stillness of the mountains. The brother who had fought against his brother was maturing now, mellowing with the years and taking a more kindly attitude toward those who had differed with him about slavery or the Union, or even about the politicians who had engineered the fratricidal war. Of course there were long to be extremists who still displayed the Confederate flag and whose faces darkened at the mention of Yankees, the Freedmen's Bureau, or carpetbaggers. But there were others in this little world in itself who were happy that the Lincoln men had won and who thought that poor old Robert Lee had somehow got mixed up on the wrong side.

Since the time of the War of the Roses the farmers of Tennessee had revolted against what they considered a conspiracy against them by big business and urban labor. But this movement found a weak response in the Smoky section, whose farmers were as individual as the irregular plots which made up their upland farms. Those in the valleys conformed more to the statewide sentiment. The cooperative movement, which had resulted in the setting up of stores and factories, had almost lost itself in the return to conventional agrarian economics. Its main results were to split the Democratic Party in the state, to the delight of the Republicans, who had control of much of East Tennessee and who could only win when there was schism in the opposing ranks.

In the bleak village of Briceville, coal miners had gone out in violent strikes against the use of convict labor in the mines. The state government wavered, promised a change, but did little except call out the militia. The mining men arose and fought the encroaching criminals, and the death of a number of the former finally aroused the state to pass laws doing away with this governmental threat to the rights of free men to labor underground. Back in the Smokies, what had been good enough for their fathers appeared to be good enough for the members of the current society, and they demonstrated their faith in the oldfashioned way by living it. A young man named Theodore Roosevelt came down from New York to do research on his *The Winning of the West,* but he created little stir among the highland dwellers, most of whom didn't know he was around. They were to appreciate better his strenuous activity later on.

Though the folks in this region lived mainly to themselves,

outsiders were being attracted to their prospering agriculture. Some of the new residents stayed, others moved on westward. In the Hickman *Pioneer* there appeared the following
bit of descriptive doggerel:

> The chigger may chig with all his might and the mocking
> bird may mock and sing, but the Tennessee crop it takes
> the cake, and the corn, you bet, is king. The crickets may
> crick and the froglets frog and the farmer sing his strain,
> for in Tennessee corn is away on top, the result of plenty
> of rain. The chinch bug may chinch and the grasshopper
> hop and the hot winds make you tire, but if anyone says
> that such things are here, just call him a terrible liar. Okla-
> homa may boom and Texas may howl and Missouri may
> shoot off her chop. But Tennessee is the place to get a
> good home and raise a great big crop.

Back in 1843 a visiting Englishman had written home that
East Tennessee offered great inducements to practical farmers,
and that "for 2,000 to 5,000 pounds, one could purchase a
princely domain." In the dawning of the twentieth century,
this was still quite true. The land which lay along the foot
of the mountains was called "mulatto land," being a dark
soil with a clay foundation. It would produce without benefit
of fertilizer forty to fifty bushels of Indians corn per acre,
or about the same amount of oats, or twenty to twenty-five
bushels of wheat. Irish potatoes, a great favorite, could be
grown at the rate of three hundred bushels to an acre. This
rich soil was from fifteen to twenty-five inches deep, light, ad-
hesive, and easily cultivated except in the "new grounds,"
which with their roots and stumps were always a tough challenge to the strength and patience of the farmers. Anyone who
can remember, as I do, the plowing in these new areas doubtless vividly recalls the kick of the plow in the stomach when

it struck a hidden root or rock, an excruciating experience that was sure to take away sleep the following night.

Small groves of trees on high spots in the cleared sections made ideal home sites, and natural springs at the foot of the slopes provided incomparably cool drinking water as well as refrigeration for the wonderfully flavorsome milk and butter. The mean annual temperature was about fifty-nine degrees, the heat of summer seldom reaching as high as ninety-four and the cold of winter rarely reaching below twenty, with only light snow lasting no more than forty-eight hours on the ground. Because of the brief winters, farmers found that there were not more than ten days in the whole year that outdoor work could not be done. This was especially important because of the crude plows, mattocks, harrows, and hoes then in use, which required so much more time in the field than modern implements. One farmer noted that he had thirty-five in his family, but the mildness of the climate had kept his doctor bill down to less than a hundred dollars over a period of five years.

For the farmer of this period there were few markets available, as well as few places where he could buy commodities, so he had to become economically independent. Such a situation could hardly provide a high scale of living. The farmer did not want it to. He purposely set his sights somewhat low, so that he would not have to work too hard and would have more leisure time. He grew no surplus, figuring on just about what would be required for him and his family and growing no more. There was little money; barter existed in the Smoky Mountain Country almost up to the time of the Second World War. A farmer would take four dozen eggs to the crossroads store and receive for them soda, salt, and some flour. His meal he had ground from the corn he had raised, carrying sacks of it on his back and walking or riding a mule through the mountains to the picturesque grist mills built over the streams, whose slow-grinding, water-propelled wheels turned out the unbolted meal used in the savory cornbread baked on his hearth or in the oven of his wood-burning stove.

Other food was largely confined to the game of the forest, a few hogs raised in rail pens or allowed to forage through the woods, an occasional beef cow or steer, the vegetables of the garden, and the greens and berries of the field. There was a strong tendency, which still spottily exists, to eat only meat and bread, the result being a lack of vitamins in the diet of the lean mountaineer — but then, he had never heard of vitamins anyway. There is little doubt, however, that his inordinate fondness for pork and pone made for an un-balanced diet and the spread of scurvy. The preponderance of starches, sweets, and grease from the excessive frying of so many foods resulted in heartburn, indigestion, hyperacidity, stomach ulcers, and even cancers. Later, county agents, aided by the great agricultural school of the University of Ten-nessee, were to go a long way in helping the people toward a properly balanced daily menu.

But few bodily ailments were brought on by nervous ten-sion or hurried work, as is too often the case nowadays. The lives of the late-nineteenth-century Smoky Mountain people were cheerful and unhurried. They saw no reason for trying to set the world on fire with ambition and furious economic struggle. The weather, good and bad, was generally accepted as the handiwork of the Lord, as were the state of the crops, business, and sometimes politics. In these people was a natural social instinct so strong and so gracious that strangers mar-veled at it. The farmer would take a few minutes off any time in the day, as would the men of the towns and cities, to chew the rag with friends. The stranger was at first — and still is — looked upon with some suspicion. As far as his worth to the community was concerned, he was not worthy until he proved himself so; but once within its graces a strong respect became apparent and a hospitality was evidenced that was at once noble and charming in its intensity. A visitor was usually asked to spend the night, and if he refused for no good reason, this was taken as a kind of rebuff. He was actually welcome to stay for weeks. Often recalled by historians is an early incident when the urbane President Martin van Buren spoke to a crowd in East Tennessee, and was later approached by an old farmer who invited him to "come over and r'ar round with the boys." Cecil Sharp, the English visitor, was impressed with the calm assurance of the mountain people, and their evident belief that they were "as good as anybody" — which indeed they were. "They have an easy and unaffected bearing," wrote Sharp, "and the unselfconscious manners of the well-bred. I have received salutations upon introductions or on bidding farewell, dignified and restrained, such as a courtier might make to his sovereign."

A tired stranger was walking through the Smoky Mountains at the end of a long day's journey. Coming around the bend of a narrow trail, he saw just ahead a log cabin from which the smoke ascended in a fine blue column straight up into the clear sky, like some Indian signal of old. Since it was almost dusk and he was still a good distance from his destination, a village hotel, the stranger approached the cabin and called out. A lean-looking man dressed in jeans and a homemade shirt ambled out onto the little porch. The stranger told him he was tired and hungry, and asked if he could buy some food. For several long moments the mountaineer regarded the stranger's face, before he made this reply:

"No, ye cain't buy anything here, stranger. But I'll give ye the best we have in the house and you're most welcome."

When a new settler arrived in a community he was immediately welcomed and supplied with all the prime necessities. He found hospitality, peace, independence, and freedom. The neighbors' children, instead of giving him and his family impudent stares and smart-aleck remarks, said "Sir" to him and "Ma'am" to his wife, and asked permission when they wanted to fondle his dog or play with his children.

When evening came, it was the home that filled the need for pleasure. As one chronicler expressed it:

> When the mountaineer's day was over, he seated himself in his homely but peaceful "mansion" and regaled his wife and weans with some old-fashioned hunters' songs, or by playing a jig upon a gourd fiddle, while his train of tatterly brats kicked up a tremendous dust as they danced over the dirt floor keeping time to the rich and mellow tones of music.

In the early part of this century a great many of the people were still illiterate (though educational strides have been made since, the illiteracy rate remains among the nation's highest). It was a common sight to see a man or woman make their mark instead of signing their names. But what they lacked in reading and writing they made up for in facile and picturesque speech. Theirs was a keen native intelligence and a wisdom largely elemental. Their constant touch with nature gave them knowledge and intuition which only outdoor people seem to have.

Their humor was sly and simple. A story is told of the halfwit who habitually frequented one of the country stores of the region. In this particular store was an old clock in ill repair which often did the unpredictable. One brisk winter day, the halfwit and a crowd of other men were seated around the pot-bellied stove in the store, as usual with the others doing all the talking. The conversation had so given way to the warm comfort that most of the group were quite sleepy. Suddenly the quietness was broken by the old clock, which proceeded to strike thirteen. The halfwit, who had not yet spoken a word, looked up, pulled his cap down over his eyes, and slowly arose.

"Well fellers," he said, "I guess I'd better be agoin', 'cause it's later than I ever knowed hit to be before."

The typical inhabitant of the region was as sensitive as he was independent. Always ready to join in a worthwhile co-operative enterprise that suited him, he was not to be forced into anything against his will. The innovations which finally came to the mountains were welcomed in some instances, resented in others. The individual quality of the uplander led him to his own way of doing things. Especially did he dislike some of the missions which were established in the mountains by Northern churches and foundations, for he discovered that in the minds of certain of his "benefactors" he and his people were being classed with heathens across the seas. John Fox, Jr., wrote that these people were:

> . . . proud, sensitive, hospitable, kindly obliging in an unreckoning way that is almost pathetic, honest, loyal in spite of their common ignorance, poverty and isolation. They are naturally capable, eager to learn, easy to uplift, Americans to the core. They make the Southern mountains a storehouse of patriotism. In themselves they are an important offset to the Old World outcasts whom we have welcomed to our shores.

In a century-old cabin which stands in the wilds of Little Greenbriar Cove, about ten miles from Gatlinburg, Tennessee, there lived for many years five single sisters of the Walker family. There were several boys in the family, and girls who married, but these five sisters loved the old home place and clung to it. As Miss Adelaide Rowell said: "They seemingly had no feminine desire to ally themselves with the male sex. No romantic moonshiner for them, they were content to spend their days in busy peace and quiet." Each sister fortunately had a special gift. One liked to weave, one was a "born gardener," one made quilts, one tied brooms and mops, and the youngest wrote poems and "ballets." Thus engaged, they spent their completely isolated lives, two of them being still alive at mid-century, the other three having passed away at ripe old ages.

For many quiet years the Walker sisters lived unto themselves, growing their own food, weaving their own clothing out of wool taken from the backs of their own sheep, cutting their own wood for heat and cooking, raising a few cows and mules for domestic use, and in general existing without need of the outside world. Then came the Great Smoky Mountains National Park. Others sold their land and moved away. Not so the Walker sisters. They fought the thing hair, tooth, and nail. Finally, touched with the pathetic, feminine nature of their pleas, the federal government granted them the right to live on their home land "until death."

A visit to the home of these celebrated sisters was illuminating. The way led along a winding, timeworn mountain trail shaded by laurel and rhododendron and thick-fringed with spreading ferns. Now and then a tiny brook crossed the road, the cold air from its clearest of waters being most refreshing. Eventually a sunlit clearing showed up ahead, in it the

Walker cabin, partly cut off from view by old trees and shrubs in the yard. The cabin was squarely built of mud-chinked logs. On its small porch soon appeared plump Miss Louise Walker, the youngest, with a handful of "ballets" she had written and was not averse to selling. Inside the one large room were the five beds in which the sisters slept. A huge fireplace was on the left, and from uncovered rafters hung everything from dried seed to ancient gourds. An old, musty smell was over the whole cabin, which in general presented a picture of somewhat untidy confusion. Old tintypes adorned the dressers, and part of the walls was covered with years-old newspapers and magazines. In the kitchen with its fireplace and cookstove sat Miss Margaret, the other and elder survivor, wrinkled but cheerful, vigorously churning one of those upright wooden dasher churns. Not far away was a loom, and behind her in the fireplace could be seen an iron kettle on a hook, simmering with greens. Fresh-canned fruit was in abundance, as well as apple butter, peach butter, and tomato preserves. Above the eating table was a huge brush made of cut-up newspapers and used at mealtime to swish away the numerous flies.

The two admitted that in recent years they had strayed a little from their self-sufficiency and bought a few "store clothes." It was late summer, and the cupboards and larders were already full in anticipation of winter, when sometimes the Walkers get snowed in. They said they loved the old, comfortable feeling of "crops gathered in and us restin' safe and snug fer a spell." These mountain women have been around for "a spell," all right, and seem as much a part of the past as the century-old cabin built by their grandfather. They are vividly typical of the satisfied, unchanging folks of this region, who desire to live much as their fathers.

The Mountain Women

In the early 1900's and for some years thereafter, most of the mountain babies were born with the assistance only of a midwife. She cost less than a doctor and, more important, was available. It mattered little to lots of families that the midwife was none too sanitary, because they were accustomed to no other way of bringing their children into the world. Often her hands were dirty, and much of her method was superstition, such as the practice of putting an axe under the bed to relieve the mother's pains. After all, a midwife was better than no assistance at all. It was in those days a custom for the expectant mother to continue her usual work up until a few days before the child was born, then be up and at her chores again almost as soon as the birth was over. For years this was considered cruel and dangerous by outsiders, until it was discovered by the medical profession that the sooner a patient can exercise herself after an operation or period of confinement, the better off she is. The mountain people have never been known for stupidity.

It is, however, a ludicrous fact that some of the uplanders did not know what caused children, in certain instances believing that birth was entirely an act of God. Such beliefs, though rare, coupled with a lack of knowledge of birth control, or the lack of belief in it, and the remoteness of most homes from drugstores and other places which dispense birth control devices, make it understandable why most of the earlier families were so large. One father whose wife had a baby just about as regularly as the year rolled around was asked why this happened. He answered: "Well, it gits purty cold up thar in the winter time and usually we jist don't have a lot else to do."

There was also a proud adherence to the customs of the referred to the long lists of children who were "begat" in the mountain people's own prolific ancestors; parents sometimes Bible, it being apparently lost sight of that in biblical times a man often had many wives instead of just one. Of no small consequence, either, was the need for many hands on the farm, and for a large number of progeny-supporters of parents in their old age. Prominent, too, was masculine pride in seeing how many offspring could be begotten, with too little regard for the welfare or looks of the woman concerned. Most of the women married in their teens, and ceaseless childbearing plus manual labor gave them prematurely aged appearances, leaving in many cases only unusually sweet voices as reminders of a still-clinging youth.

A local father who had twenty-two children went to church one Sunday and was asked by a friend. "Bill, you've got a mighty big family, aintcha?"

"Yes," was the studied reply. "The Lord says fer us to multiply and 'plenish the earth."

The other looked straight at him. "But Bill," he said, "the Lord didn't mean fer you to try to do hit all."

Illegitimacy existed not so much from intent as from circumstance. There was an utter lack of privacy in the homes, and the old joke about the guest being compelled from lack of room to sleep with the farmer's daughter had more basis of truth than has been generally realized. This living together day and night gave the children an early knowledge of the sex relationship which sometimes lent hospitality a promiscuous turn. Furthermore, up until the 1920's there were many couples living in the mountains who were not legally married.

The inconvenience of journeying to a justice of the peace or the long wait before the itinerant preacher came around led to consummation without benefit of conventional sanctions — and in some circles, little was thought of it.

The work which the women did was nothing short of amazing. The daily routine ran something like this: up with the rooster's crow at daybreak, into the kitchen to cook a breakfast of bacon, biscuits, and gravy, in the meanwhile taking care of what children were awake. A quick washing of the dishes, then a dash to the fields to cultivate or gather the crops. Return at noon to cook and serve a heavy lunch of vegetables, side-meat, and cornbread. In the afternoon, more work in the fields; then back in time to cook the evening meal of ham, vegetables, milk, and homemade jelly. After supper, the mountain wife carried water to the house from the spring, which might be a quarter of a mile away, and then chopped up wood for the fires the next morning. With dark, she washed the dishes again, put the children to bed, sewed or quilted awhile in the chimney corner, then rested her weary self in bed. On special days, such as Saturdays and Sundays, she picked fruit from the trees, went in search of wild berries, canned or dried fruit, and maybe managed to work in a quick visit with the neighbor over the hill. No wonder this made her look old before her time. Her clothes did not help her appearance, either. They usually consisted of a sunbonnet over a calico or gingham dress. Some of the women used snuff, some, when very old, smoked pipes. The garb of the husband ordinarily was "overhalls," comfortable, cheap, and easily washed garments. In winter he wore long underwear, and slept in it until forced by sanitary reasons to change, perhaps once a month. His shoes were brogans with leather laces, and he usually wore no socks except in cold weather. In summer, wide-brimmed, slouch straw hats were worn by both sexes, comfortably shading even if virtually hiding the faces of the wearers. In the other months, shapeless, rounded black felts gave their wearers the name of "wool hats."

One spring, just before the First World War, a pretty East Tennessee girl, upon completing school, received as her graduation present a new hoe tied with a colorful ribbon. The very next day she was out in the fields using this present, along with her father, brothers, and sisters, for it was the height of spring and the crops had to be cultivated quickly before "the weeds got 'em." She took it all in good spirit, though. She knew that her parents did not want her to have to do such work always, for they too had advanced in their thinking and had become more educated as the century wore on. Their gift to her in the way of advice and inspiration was their desire for her to have a better life than they; but with the new things she might attain, they hoped she would still hold on to the good things of the past — religious devotion, loyalty, sincerity, respect for parents, family, friends, and for herself.

Three important symbols of the lingering frontier life were the fireplace, the ash hopper, and the gourd. Traditionally the fireplace took up most of one end of the cabin and served for heat, light, and cooking. When mealtime approached, the housewife would rake out on the hearth a glowing mass of embers, and place over them the covered cast-iron oven known as a "baker." At the moment when the heat was just right, she would remove the heavy lid with an iron poker and cover its upturned edges with live coals. Inside the hot baker, now well greased with butter or lard, she next would place a thick batch of cornbread dough.

Sometimes "cracklings," as toasted meat skins were called, were used as shortening, giving a speckled appearance and a delicious nutty flavor to the bread. As soon as the bread was taken from the baker, it was eaten steaming hot with butter and milk. Often it was simply crumbled into a glass of milk and eaten with a spoon, this delectable dish being called "crumble up" and often serving as the sole item in a full evening meal by the mellow fire. And bread was only one of the many uses of the fireplace for cooking, which included green beans or turnip greens cooked with pork, cabbage boiled with ham hocks, "poke salet" made from the young shoots of pokeweed, and similar dishes cooked in kettles, and cobbler pies baked for dessert.

Ash hoppers, such as the one which stood in the backyard of my grandparents' house, were another domestic institution. Here and there one may still be found in the older homes of the Smokies. The hopper consisted of triangular trough cut in a small log, one end of which was then raised a few inches, and a frame set on four posts in the ground with its peak in the trough. Wood ashes from the kitchen stove or fireplace were poured into the hopper, and kept under cover until soap-making time. Water was then allowed to drip over the ashes, and after going through it trickled into the trough in the form of lye, which was collected in a big kettle and boiled with pieces of fat meat. The resulting soft brown substance was lye soap, and as soon as it became dry enough it was cut into pieces with a knife. Many thought it better than store-bought soap.

Gourds were grown by every mountain family and reached large size at times, some of them holding as much as two gallons. They were utilized as containers for lard, sugar, salt, soap, syrup, molasses, and seed. With holes of sufficient size cut in them, the gourds could be used as birdhouses; many a barnyard was set off by a cluster of these gourd-houses fastened high on a pole and surrounded by flying martins, swallows, or blackbirds which had built their nests therein. Hardly a spring of water but had its drinking gourd used as a dipper by all-comers, with a small hole cut in the end of the "handle" through which passed a bit of bindertwine to hold it on a bush. Even nowadays some of the oldtimers say that no water can possibly taste as good as that of a cold spring quaffed from a gourd on a hot day.

Superstitions

The very nature of the Great Smoky Mountains suggests superstition. The high peaks are mysterious and lonely, the ridges indefinite in their lengths; and the deep coves below appear to be the perfect abodes of spirits from another world.

From the time when the white settlers first came to this region and caught some of the mysticism of the Indians, superstition has surrounded the lives of the mountain people. Some of the strange beliefs have meaning only to the oldest residents, who sit on their cabin porches and tell you of them while they look at the distant mountaintops with a faraway expression in their eyes. Others are still believed in and even practised by the younger people, though they may have moved away from the mountains to some prosperous valley.

It is not possible to analyze or classify all these quaint beliefs within the compass of this book; we can only list some of the principal superstitions of a storied country where probably more abound than in any other part of the nation.

To cure headache, blow tobacco smoke in each ear. To

cure chickenpox, have the person with the pox lie down on the ground and run some chickens over him. To stop a baby's slobbering, go to the brook and get a minnow and let the baby suck the minnow's tail. For rheumatism, take the bark of a cherry tree and put it in corn whiskey and drink it. Keep a flannel string around the body to keep away disease. To have good luck with baby chicks, throw the hatched eggshells over a housetop. Anybody who has hairy legs is said to be a good hog raiser. The twenty-seventh day of August is the "most poisonest" day of the year. If you sing at the table, it is bad luck. Ring around the moon, rain soon; ring around the sun, rain none. If it rains while the sun is shining, it will be raining at the same time the next day.

Hiccups are immediately cured by angering the patient or by throwing cold water in his face. Sores on the feet in the fall are due to the poison of dog days in the summer, and can be cured by a fat-meat poultice. Colic can be relieved by rubbing the stomach with a bone from a hog's foot. Warts may be removed by rubbing each wart with a bean split open, and burying the bean halves under the drip of the house for seven days. When beads of sweat do not stand on a cow's nose, the cow is sick. Perhaps she has lost her cud; if so, a cud can be made for her from cherry bark, poke leaves, and coarse bran. Sunday is the best day to start weaning a calf. The goose bone is used as a seasonal barometer: if the coloring near the point is dark and extended, a rough winter is ahead.

Colorful Religion

Around 1800 a great religious revival swept the Smoky Mountain Country and had a tremendous effect upon the habits of the people. Its manifestations were numerous, but most remarkable were the physical reactions of the converts. A large number in some sects gave way to peculiar motions known as "the jerks." Sometimes a person was affected in one part of the body, sometimes in another. The head would jerk backward or forward or from side to side so quickly that it was difficult to distinguish the features. Persons were seen to sway forward and backward almost to the floor without falling, saying later that this was one of the happiest experiences of their lives. Some laughed continuously, others fell exhausted from running around. A story is told of an old Presbyterian preacher of East Tennessee who had gone into the woods to pray and was seized by the jerks. He happened to be standing near a sapling, so he caught hold of it to steady himself. His head began to jerk backward and forward, then it turned upward and he gave out loud grunting sounds. A wit who once found him in this odd position reported that he had discovered the old minister barking up a tree.

Such actions of a century and a half ago may seem in present times to be only folk history. But they are not confined to yesteryear. A sect was founded in 1909 by George Hensley, who, in his fervor, handled rattlesnakes. He based his actions on *Mark* 16:18, which states, "They shall take up serpents." The converts to this sect are nearly always among the more illiterate mountain people. They do not believe in wearing neckties, since these adornments are not mentioned in the Bible. They likewise refuse to wear eyeglasses or take medicine. When greeting each other, the men kiss the men, the women the women. In September, 1945, in the little East Tennessee community of Dolly Pond, a man named Lewis F. Ford died from the bite of a rattler he had handled during the religious services of the sect. Members of the cult were arrested and fined. A few months later, another man, Clint Jackson of Daisy, Tennessee, died under the same circumstances. By this time, people were so generally aroused that the state government passed a law forbidding the handling of snakes in religious ceremonies. This legislation virtually stopped the gruesome practice, although occasionally there comes a report of some person so excited by these revivalist rites that he has grabbed a reptile, and to the tune of weird guitar music by the light of hot oil lamps which the other brethren have handled with their bare hands to show their devotion, has received the fatal bite.

At Cleveland, Tennessee, is the world headquarters of the Church of God, an unusual organization whose various divisions claim a total of one hundred thousand congregations in every state in the Union and in all parts of the world. Not so extreme as some sects, this church, which grew out of the mountains of Tennessee and North Carolina, nevertheless believes in some practices which are not generally orthodox and which have been ridiculed as coming within the category of Holy Rolling.

The Church of God was founded in 1903 by A. J. Tomlinson, a salesman for the American Bible Society. He had visited a little church in Cherokee County, North Carolina, known as the Holiness Church at Camp Creek, and was impressed with its teachings. So when he moved across the mountains to Tennessee, he organized a similar church at Union Grove, near Cleveland in Bradley County. In 1908 the church he had founded was spreading into numerous congregations, so Tomlinson established the headquarters of the organization at Cleveland and "received the baptism of the spirit, attested by the use of unknown tongues." By 1922

he had become a bishop, but was charged with misappropria-
tion of church funds and ousted. Tomlinson took his case to
court and was exonerated. He forthwith founded his own
branch of the Church of God, became its general overseer,
and expanded it throughout the world. The small tabernacle
which had been erected in Cleveland was subsequently enlarged until it now seats over five thousand delegates, who
come from all over the earth to attend the annual conventions. These meetings are enlivened by the talking in tongues,
by participants jumping up and down, clapping their hands,
and shouting "Hallelujah" and "Amen" in response to the
minister, by feet washing and much literal quoting of the
Bible.

J. R. Kinser, general treasurer of a major division of the
church, explained that the talking in unknown tongues
sometimes means in "foreign" tongues, that is, in the native
languages spoken by delegates from the foreign countries.
Kinser told this writer that he himself was once caught up
by the power of the Lord and found himself speaking a
tongue which some said was French, although he had never
studied this language. He told, in apparent deep sincerity,
of another man, a member of the church, who was praying
on his knees when suddenly the power of God "literally
lifted him up in the air and he floated around the room."
He told also of his brother-in-law, who had been gassed in
World War I and also had injuries to his feet and legs. So
serious were his ailments that he became disheartened and
started from Tennessee to California to die. While passing
through Chattanooga, he happened to stop at a meeting being held in a little Church of God, and was healed — all this
after the doctors had given him up. Kinser was asked if the
"jerks" were manifestations of the power of God, and he

said they were. He explained: "If God wants your hand up in the air, why he just puts it there."

In 1943 the eventful career of A. J. Tomlinson came to an end — he who had worn a rubber collar to prevent wilting during his fervent sermons, who had traveled as much as fifty-five thousand miles a year by train, boasting that he never took a Pullman because by riding in a day coach he saved money for the Lord, who was said to have personally signed the ministerial credentials of one hundred thousand preachers. Following his death a scramble for his position ensued between his two sons, Bishop M. A. Tomlinson, thirty-seven, of Cleveland, and Bishop Homer A. Tomlinson, fifty-one, of New York City. Homer contended that he had been selected by his father to lead the church, but Southern members had been suspicious of the "city slicker" tendencies of Homer and wanted his younger brother to head the organization. The church split, leaving one headquarters in Cleveland, another in New York headed by Homer (who in 1951 decided to run for President of the United States — by fasting), and still a third in Chattanooga. There are still other offshoots of the Church of God, such as the congregation known as the Outpouring of the Latter Day Rain, in Los Angeles; the Jesus Only Church in Harlem, New York City; the Remnant Church of God in Lansing, Michigan; the Non-Digressive Church of God; the Justified Church of God; and the Glorified Church, which advances money to pay the debts of all new members. In general, members of the church do not touch tobacco, liquor, or playing cards, and refrain from dancing, professional ball games, and the wearing of jewelry. Stress is laid on abstaining from fornication, and members believe that a divorced person should not marry as long as his or her ex-spouse is alive. The Church of God also believes that the millennium is not far off.

Eighteen miles west of Murphy, North Carolina, on Highway 294 is an impressive outdoor spectacle among the forested mountains known as the Fields of the Wood — a series of gigantic figures and markers in white concrete representing biblical symbols of the Church of God, and designed to commemorate the birth of the church, which was founded here by Tomlinson in 1903. Officials of the church call attention to the fact that this event occurred exactly six months and four days before the Wright Brothers made their famous first airplane flight at Kitty Hawk, also in North Carolina. Now from a modern plane, or from the ground, one can see the Ten Commandments laid out in huge white letters on a five-acre slope of the mountain, topped off by a fifty-foot-high figure representing the New Testament. Great arches, altars, crosses, and other religious monuments on the adjoining hills startle the passerby and inspire the church members. The gargantuan tableau, whose purpose is to impress visitors with the words of the Bible, is maintained by the M. A. Tomlinson Church of God with headquarters in Cleveland, and its name comes from the passage in the 132nd Psalm which states, regarding the habitation of the Lord: "We found it in the fields of the wood."

Ham and Tobacco

Rapidly taking its place alongside the famous Virginia ham, Smithfield ham, Canadian bacon, and other such delicacies is the Tennessee country ham. This particular kind of meat is nothing new. It began with John Sevier and his mountain country long before most states had names, much less favorite hams. But the Tennessee variety, which originated in the uplands of its eastern portion, was for a long time confined to the private knowledge and palates of the settlers who prepared it. It is an unusual kind of ham and still may only be found, outside the South, in restaurants which specialize in rare viands. Not everyone likes it. As with gamy venison or bitter caviar, enjoyment waits until a taste for it has been developed. To those raised on its salty goodness, however, it is the supreme delicacy among meats and the ultimate in eating.

Even in the Smoky Mountains, Tennessee country ham is not often found in the markets or corner groceries. Now and then one may see it advertised, or an occasional restaurant may include it on the menu. But most of it is safely ensconced in the oldfashioned smokehouses of the farms, far back from the traveler's view, and regarded as so valuable that it is not for sale. Being able to buy the real country ham is almost like knowing somebody who knows a bootlegger of "genuine corn liquor."

The ham is cured just as it was in the old days. Hog-killin' time was then and still is an important festivity. The neighbors gather at the farmhouse to spend the day and collectively perform the hog-killing jobs. The same group usually takes turns at each farm in the neighborhood, repeating the same rites from day to day until the hogs have all been disposed of.

Early in the morning, their breaths fogging through the crisp November air, the farmers set forth, part of them to the hog lot, the rest to build a roaring fire under a huge oblong kettle half-filled with water. For killing, some prefer to stand with a rifle in front of the hog, properly fattened from pighood especially for this occasion, and "let him have it" right between the eyes; following which he is stuck in the throat with a long knife. Often the method of "sticking" is used alone, without the shooting. The hog is then allowed to bleed as long as possible.

By this time the water in the big kettle is scalding hot, about one hundred fifty degrees, and the carcass is lifted in. The hair is scraped off, and the scalded hog is hung up on a sort of scaffold where his body is slit open with a sharp butcher knife, the insides taken out, and the whole carcass rinsed with cold water. The meat is next allowed to chill but not to freeze. The ideal temperature for this process is thirty-four degrees, although up to forty is satisfactory. If allowed to freeze, the meat will not be as good because of the undesirable effects of too-quick freezing of the bones.

After being cut up into hams, shoulders, head, sides, ribs, and backbone, the pork is prepared for curing. But before this is done, there is usually a fine feast of backbone and ribs for all present, these two fresh items being broiled to a turn and served dripping with grease, a delicacy fit for a king, if not particularly healthy as a steady diet. Fresh sausage is also made, with spices including pepper and sage, and put away in long round sacks or canned for future use, though generous portions of the new product are usually eaten immediately. Head cheese, known as "souse meat," is made from the head, jowls, and brains.

Although there are newer methods of curing the hams, such as that employing sugar, saltpeter, and fancy peppers, the oldfashioned way, which produces the genuine Tennessee country ham, is simply to bury the hams in a small mountain of salt and let them stay there for a month. They are then hung up in the smokehouse, where they stay until eaten. Some prefer to smoke their hams in hickory smoke, others just take them straight. The result of this process is a rich, red, salty ham, which when fried in its own grease with a small amount of black coffee added for mottling and seasoning, and served with plenty of very hot biscuits over which the red-eye gravy is poured, produces an epicure's dream in the estimation of any southerner who has been raised up on it.

Tobacco is the oldest staple cash crop in the South. Its extensive growing came somewhat late to the Smoky Mountain region, but it has now assumed large proportions in the agricultural and social pattern, partly because so much hand labor is still required to raise it. Of the three main kinds of tobacco raised in the United States — cigar leaf, burley, and bright-yellow — the last-named is the most important because from it cigarettes are made. This kind of tobacco grows best on thin yellowish or white soil, much of which is found in East Tennessee and western North Carolina. After cigarettes became popular, the local farmers began raising the bright-yellow tobacco on their hitherto wornout land. They found that by adding the right amount of the right fertilizers they could get a successful yield from this land; and so great was their output that tobacco prices soon went down. But after the First World War these farmers began planning their crops better, growing less tobacco and getting more for it. North Carolina is still the largest tobacco-growing state, but neighboring East Tennessee, just across the Smoky Mountains, has come a long way in tobacco raising.

The importance of the bright-leaf tobacco in these people's lives is evidenced by the increasing number of tobacco farms and warehouses which meet the visiting eye. Machines can do little of the work in growing the tobacco; most of it is raised by hand. As in cotton growing, women and children are widely utilized. Some large-scale tobacco growers use machines to plant the tiny shoots, but even then the men who ride the conveyors must actually set out the young tobacco plants by hand. The smaller grower has no conveyor to begin with, so he bends his back to do it all. In early summer the maturing tobacco plants must be topped and the suckers removed, all by hand. Spraying against worms or removing them by hand are usually done by the women and children. The gathering of the tobacco, curing it, and preparing it for market are also done by hand — by skillful hands. Toward the end of summer the leaves are stripped from the plants and placed on sleds which take them to the barns. The leaves are then tied in bunches and hung over sticks, the sticks placed on racks, and curing is under way.

The bright-leaf tobacco of the region is cured in special barns with furnaces built into the walls. From the pipes or flues branching out from the furnaces, around the dirt floor, heat is carried to all parts of the barn, thus drying the tobacco. Wood fires heat the furnaces, and must be kept burning day and night at just the right temperature. During this curing period, when so many of the folks have to gather anyway, social activities are engaged in by those who watch and keep the fires burning. Beside the curing barns, crowds gather with their banjos and guitars in the twilight hours and sing or dance, play games, talk politics, or just gossip. Over all is the rich, sweet smell of the drying tobacco, the weed of peace which the Indians once smoked here in their long pipes.

After being cured, the tobacco is tied in uniform bunches known as "hands," loaded into wagons or trucks, and hauled to a warehouse, where it is sold. The farmer must pay for the cost of selling, and does not know what his bright-leaf

will bring until it is bought. The resonant chant of the tobacco auctioneer is a sort of swan song to the many days of
long, hard work which are required to make this "music."

Aluminum and Copper

Soon after the turn of the century, the economy of the
Smoky Mountain Country was given a boost by the development of mining and smelting. Near historic Maryville, in one
of the most picturesque foothill sections, the Aluminum Company of America completed its sprawling works, which was
to become the largest aluminum manufacturing center in
the world. Local people flocked to the big new plant for
jobs, and found some of the hot operations of rolling out
sheets of aluminum a sharp contrast to the cool atmosphere
of their native Smokies. But the pay was higher and that
counted for a lot. The native deposits of bauxite ore, which
is used in extracting aluminum, and the proximity of cheap
water power made the operation of the forty-acre smelting
plant profitable from the start.

At the present time the traveler on U.S. Highway 64 comes
upon a barren waste in this usually fertile mountain country
that literally looks like hell. For a space of many miles, a man-
made desert of twenty-three thousand acres stretches. Not a
single tree, bird, or blade of grass are in sight. The land is
dead. Across the reddish, dreary badland, deep gullies cut
through the eroded earth, and here and there ramshackle
houses cling to the edges of the forsaken soil. This is the country around Ducktown, center of East Tennessee's copper
basin. The town of Ducktown itself, like Copperhill, its twin
township, is a prosperous community. On a rise nearby the

huge buildings and tall smokestacks of the copper smelter loom grimly over the prostrate land.

This barren ground was caused by man's predatory eagerness to grab what he could from the earth quickly and without proper thought of the consequences. He has learned his lesson since, but the damage is already done. The copper mining which was begun here a century ago partly involved roasting the ore in large open piles to get rid of the sulphur content. This process required much wood, so the trees in the surrounding forests were cut down. Then the smoke from the roasting ore, full of sulphur dioxide, settled upon the nearby vegetation and killed it all. By the time the roasting process was stopped, in 1904, the trees had disappeared from the Ducktown area. It had also been a practice each year to burn off the sedge grass which for centuries had kept the ground from washing away, and this, along with the effects of the chemicals, led to the eventual death of the grass, which in turn brought on destructive erosion and gullies. At one point, in an effort to allay the damage, a four-hundred-foot chimney was built onto the smelter high on the mountains; but by this time the harm had already been done.

Up until 1908, the only product of the basin was copper. That year the Tennessee Copper Company, which operates the mines, began the manufacture of sulphuric acid from the sulphur dioxide smoke, and to its amazement learned that this not only eliminated the harmful smoke, but that the product was worth more than the copper itself. Since this discovery, the smoke no longer is released.

Although the extent of the copper basin is about one hundred square miles, the copper deposits are confined to an area only six miles long and four miles wide. Before the Second World War a fine program of reforestation was being carried out here by the TVA and the copper company, but only five per cent of the area had been replanted with trees when this activity was interrupted by the war. The shock which a person feels when coming upon this gigantic earth-scar for the first time gives emphasis to the need for resuming the program. Besides the wasted land, the only reminder of mining in the early days is a small brick chimney on one of the hills near Ducktown. This lone sentry stands as a reminder that once a great forest covered the region, and some day, with proper action, may stand here again.

VI

The "Volunteer State"

THE "Volunteer State" is no idle sobriquet attached to Tennessee by some visionary with dreams of willing valor. It is a nickname earned the hard way. Said by most historians to have originated in the Mexican War, the designation really sprang fullfledged at the birth of the state itself — which is another way of saying that it began with the oldest section, East Tennessee.

The men of these mountains fought their way into the wilderness and then struggled against heavy odds to build a free society out of primitive conditions. They volunteered for King's Mountain, Horseshoe Bend, and New Orleans. Sevier and Jackson often had so many volunteers that they had to send a part of them home with thanks. When Tennessee's James K. Polk as President declared war against Mexico in 1846 and asked for 50,000 volunteers, the state which had sent him to the political forefront came forward itself with 30,000 eager men, although its quota was only 2800. About 5000 of these were accepted, and served with distinction from Monterrey to Chapultepec. Tennessee was the last state to leave the Union, the first to return. She gave the South more soldiers than any other Southern state, and the Union more than any other of the Confederate group. In the Spanish-American War, the state early furnished more than its share of volunteers, a number of whom were Rough Riders from East Tennessee who rode with Teddy Roosevelt at San Juan Hill. According to the records, McMinn County in East Tennessee furnished more volunteers per capita than any other county in the United States in the First World War. In the Second, and in the Korean conflict, the Volunteer State has well upheld the record which won for it its name. The U.S. Army Recruiting Service figured out, in the Second World War, that "the ideal composite soldier" came from the South, had volunteered, and that because of his natural background and hardy American ancestry had within himself a wholehearted desire to fight for his country and was thus the prime example of the American fighting man.

In the World War, the 30th Division, composed largely of Tennesseans, was given credit in the report of Field Marshal Sir Douglas Haig for being the first troops to break the supposedly impregnable Hindenburg Line. Wrote Haig:

> Ninety per cent of the men were pure Anglo-Saxon. No division is so truly American, if generations of ancestry on our soil count for being American. . . . Tall, lean and corn-fed, when the King of England came to the front, they marshalled a company of the tallest as an example of American manhood, with impressive results. . . . Silent and polite men, used to solitudes, thinking definitely and simply in old-fashioned terms of life and death, they were touched with the crusade spirit from their very origin more sentimentally and more intensely than dwellers in the cities.

In the Tennessee mountains, not far from the birthplace of Cordell Hull, lived an uneducated farmer named Alvin

C. York who, though strongly religious, was a crack shot when it came to shooting squirrels out of the high trees with a rifle. He was a devout Christian, superintendent of a Sunday school in the village of Pall Mall. But when he went into the 328th Infantry Regiment of the 82nd ("All American") Division, he apparently took as his guidance the admonishment of the Lord when he told David to smite his enemies with the sword. In the Argonne Forest on October 8, 1918, York, armed only with an Enfield rifle and a pistol and using some German prisoners as a screen, picked off and killed, one by one, twenty Germans, captured one hundred thirty-two including three lieutenants and a major, and put thirty-five machine guns out of action. Though the biggest, this was only one of York's exploits during the war. His action thwarted the efforts of an entire battalion that was planning to counterattack. For his bravery, he was awarded the Congressional Medal of Honor, the Distinguished Service Cross, and the explicit thanks of Congress. General Pershing said that Alvin York was the outstanding soldier of the war. When he returned to his lowly home, the hero was presented with the finest farm in the county by his appreciative neighbors and friends. Since then he has lived the quiet life of the country squire, taking time out to found a school and in recent years to bring in two oil wells in his county.

Prohibition and Moonshine

Agitation for Prohibition had been growing in Tennessee for years, reaching an early climax in the eastern part of the state with the founding of Harriman, the first "industrial-prohibition city" of the nation, in 1890. A man named Fred-erick Gate of New York originated the idea. He felt that industrial progress was motivated largely by temperance, so he persuaded Professor A. A. Hopkins and General Clinton B. Fisk, two prominent prohibitionists, to help him establish an enterprise to prove this theory. The result was the East Tennessee Land Company, which was organized in October of 1889 and bought several thousand acres of land on the site of the present city of Harriman. On February 26, 1890, an auction was held at which, in three days, three hundred lots were sold for a total of $600,000. About three thousand prospects, largely preachers and prohibitionists, were on hand, representing a score of states. Unique in each of the deeds was the "no saloon clause," which provided that the purchaser would not use the land or allow it to be used for the purpose of manufacturing, storing, or selling intoxicating liquors as a beverage. Should the property be so used, the deed was automatically nullified and the land would revert to the company. According to available records, no land sold in the project was ever lost for this reason.

Within two years, eight churches were flourishing in the new community, and from the start the members of the Women's Christian Temperance Union were busy as the proverbial bees. Temperance Temple was established, the only thing of its kind in the South. This spacious edifice had a large auditorium for general meetings and entertainment of religious and temperance organizations. The moneychangers got into this temple, however, for within a few years the ladies had to sell it to discharge their financial obligations. Though the project turned out to be an industrial failure after the depression of 1893, "it was always considered a moral success."

*   *   *

Apparently there wasn't much more profit in moonshine either. A hard and glamorless job, it was most indulged in by the poorest folks, whose stills, instead of being those elaborate affairs shown in cartoons, were mainly tub mills which managed to grind a "tub full of corn" that had been surreptitiously carried over the rough mountains at night. The crude stills were usually hidden under the brush in some cove near a creek, and operated under conditions which made for insanitation. Sometimes, to hasten the distilling process or to give the liquor a brighter color or faster bead, the moonshiners would use a little lye or buckeyes or even tobacco juice. These ingredients, of course, were far from beneficial to the insides of those who drank the moonshine.

In early days the stuff sold for two dollars a gallon, but, like everything else, inflation was to hit this business too. The small profits made were given as the main reason for distilling the illicit liquor; the poorer farmers complained that the long mountain trails and lack of means of transportation made the raising of corn unprofitable unless part of it was used for distilling. As far as violence went, the moonshiners nearly always ran rapidly away at the approach of any stranger to their stills, and rarely did they shoot unless cornered, any such resort being mainly to scare away the intruder rather than kill him.

(Actually, the most cherished drink of the people in general was cold spring water, and they developed what amounted to almost a fetish about its quality. When, later, a lot of the mountain settlers moved to the lowlands, they would not, for a long time, drink the well, cistern, or hydrant water that was available. My own father had a devoted attachment to his habit of getting good, cold natural spring water to drink, and would talk about it as if it were the rarest nectar. It was his strongest drink.)

In the years during which our national government made constitutional efforts to prohibit intoxicating liquors, the undertaking had much success in East Tennessee. The reaction to this statement by a New Yorker or Chicagoan accustomed to moonshining stories is usually open-mouthed skepticism. Nevertheless, official statistics, as well as the testimony of the residents, tend to bear out its truthfulness.

Not that moonshining or drinking were entirely stopped. The former went right on, as it does at the present time, although it operated on perhaps a lesser scale. As has been pointed out, the mores of the mountaineers did not change as rapidly as those of their less-sequestered neighbors, and this certainly applied to the making of illegal liquor. But in the average rural and small-town community during the 'twenties, cases of public drunkenness were rare, and anyone who habitually drank to excess was looked upon by the great majority of citizens as "trash." The reason for the lack of insobriety was simple. There were few bootleggers and no speakeasies in the small communities, and it was therefore hard to get liquor — so hard, in fact, that most people would not go to the trouble and risk of obtaining it, even though they might have been inclined to drink some had it been convenient.

As to the extent of moonshining, it is interesting to note that, according to the official government figures, the number of stills seized in Tennessee decreased from 1612 in 1929, to 991 in 1933, the last year of Prohibition. The number of gallons of mash confiscated dropped from 1,999,375 in 1929 to 656,950 in 1933, and the number of persons arrested for moonshining fell from 2591 in the former year to 1723 in the latter. By 1950, it was enlightening to find, 1109 stills were seized in the state, a slight rise from the Prohibition year of 1933. So it seems the Eighteenth Amendment did have some effect in the Smoky Mountains.

Tales of the "revenoors and 'leggers" always make interesting yarns for the visitors to the section. There is the one about the small son of the mountaineer who was accosted by a revenue officer.

"Where's your father?" asked the officer.

"Pappy's up at the still."

"Where's your mother?"

"She's up at the still too."

"I'll give you a dollar," said the officer, "if you will take me up there."

"All right," said the boy, "give me the dollar."

"I'll give it to you when we get back," said the officer.

"No sir, mister, give it to me now," insisted the boy. "You ain't a-comin' back."

In some Southern towns the buying and drinking of moonshine liquor has become a sort of tradition. People of the rural districts are inclined to be tolerant, because some of their families have patronized moonshining since the times of their forefathers. One funeral I attended was observed with due solemnity, but afterward the host called the men present aside, told them they had been under a strain, and gave those who desired it a large swig from his bottle of moonshine.

The courts are apt to be lenient in the case of bootleggers. Violators in the rural districts are usually put on probation several times before they are given sentences, in the meantime making enough money from 'legging for their fines, plus a neat, untaxed balance. Some bootleggers figure probable nabbings by "the men," as they call the Federal Alcohol Tax Unit personnel, in their tentative budgets, allowing a certain estimated loss for future fines.

One reason for the increase of bootlegging even without Prohibition seems to be that more profit can be made in this way than by selling legal liquor. One mountain bootlegger had to shut down for a time, and for a revealing reason. There was plenty of legal spirits on sale in his town, but the local tipplers wanted their corn whiskey. The moonshiner was faced with a temporary shortage of his regular product, so he had to buy legal liquor, run it through activated charcoal to remove the color, and resell it to his customers as moonshine until he could replenish his regular supply. Another 'legger was caught pouring legal whiskey into a plain jug so he could sell it as moonshine, his explanation being that he could sell it for more that way.

The International Correspondence Schools had as a pupil a young East Tennessee mountaineer who was doing very well in his course in metal-working. He sent in his lessons regularly, but a time came when he was not heard from for several months. The school checked up and found he had a new address — the state prison. He wrote the I.C.S. a letter begging the officials not to be ashamed of him. It seems that during his trial as a moonshiner, his corn whiskey still had been brought into the courtroom as evidence. The judge and jury examined it carefully. "They all thought it was the finest copper-welding job they had ever seen," he wrote with pride, "and I owe it all to I.C.S."

Just before this writing, I was discussing the subject of moonshine with an Eastern acquaintance, who told me a story about an experience he had had. I reproduce his account more or less verbatim:

"I set forth on my quest in a Smoky Mountain town whose name I respectfully will not mention. I started down the main street and stopped the first young man I met. Where, I demanded, could I find some real oldtime corn whiskey?

" 'You mean moonshine?'

"I nodded.

"He then told me of a certain taxi driver, down the street three blocks and off to the left one, who, he said, might be able to help. Soon I was at the spot, glancing somewhat furtively around; and sure enough, there was the taxi driver seated comfortably in his idle cab. I edged over and quietly made known my desire. He nodded stoically, as if such a query was routine, and informed me that the price was $2.50 a pint — good stuff, too. Of course, he knew people had told stories about dead rats having been found in stills, that fusel oil had been known to be used in making moonshine, as well as lye, kerosene, and wood alcohol; but this didn't worry him, since he personally didn't touch the stuff.

"After some reflection, I reached for my wallet and told him I'd take a pint.

" 'Oh, I ain't got it,' he said.

"Seems he hadn't handled any moonshine for years. But right up the street, four blocks and down one, there was another taxi driver near a filling station who undoubtedly had some. I thanked him and drove on.

"It appeared to me a smart idea to buy some gasoline at the filling station in question, thus making the negotiation come more naturally. The attendant proving to be friendly, I asked him which cab driver was my man. He pointed to a squat, heavy-set individual with an overhanging stomach which looked promisingly like the end product of a corn-whiskey diet, and allowed he might be the one. He further allowed, at my urgent request, that he would talk to the driver on the subject of moonshine.

"The two stood at some distance from me and talked in low tones for several minutes, now and then casting a glance in my direction. I felt quite prominent. Occasionally the taxi driver would lower his head and look at me sidewise from under the edge of his cap bill. Finally the attendant came back to my car. It would take several minutes, he announced, but the driver had gone after moonshine.

"Forty-five minutes later, no taxi driver had shown up with any bottle. The attendant said he couldn't understand it. He admitted that the taxi driver had been afraid I was a 'revenoor,' but that he had assured him I was not. It was getting late in the afternoon, so I said I'd have to be going. The attendant apologized. Then he told me of another taxi stand, down the street six blocks and over three.

"Six blocks down and over three — I was getting determined — I found two men sitting on their haunches against the side of a store building near where their cabs were parked, leisurely whittling on pieces of wood. They listened poker-faced to my request, then looked meaningly at each other for a long time without saying a word. I changed my request to a plea — came right out and explained that I was no 'revenoor,' and would they please not be afraid of me?

"The two now began to talk in low tones to each other. One was a mature individual with a long, serious face; the other a youth hardly out of his teens. I moved back so they could converse privately. The older one finally looked sidewise at me and gave a reserved nod. The younger one arose and came toward me, his face slightly flushed.

" 'Well mister,' he said grimly, 'if you're the law, ye better shoot straight, 'cause I'm agoin' to git it fer ye!'

"I smiled and tried to look reassuring. He got into his cab and roared out of the stand. He'd be gone about half an hour, said the older man quietly. I started to get back in my car to wait it out, but he looked as if he'd prefer my staying right with him — and not straying toward any possible telephone or policeman — so I stayed. We talked of the weather and the high price of hamburgers. It seemed as if the young fellow would never return.

"But finally he reappeared, stopped his car, looked carefully around, and then got out carrying something in a small brown-paper poke. He walked slowly toward us, saying not a word, and, instead of handing it to me, laid the package down on a small bench out of sight behind his car. I maneuvered slowly over and laid hands on the bottle inside, and from the look of the clear liquid it was the real thing, all right. Then I reached for my pocketbook. The young man drew suddenly back, a sharp, hard look coming into his eyes. I realized that he thought I was reaching for a gun.

"Unfreezing, I laughed with real heartiness, paid him, and went on my way rejoicing. There's nothing like corn whiskey."

Women and Votes

The summer of 1920 was an exciting time in the political lives of American women. For years, under militant leaders, they had battled for the right to vote, and it seemed that their hopes were about to be realized. Thirty-five states had already ratified the Nineteenth Amendment to the Constitution, and it needed thirty-six to become law. By an odd combination of circumstances, there was no chance for any state except Tennessee to ratify the amendment before the presidential election of 1920, so Tennessee had become the center of national attention. And as usual, it fell to East Tennessee to play a decisive part.

Governor A. H. Roberts was being urged from all sides to call a special session of the state legislature. Finally, after President Woodrow Wilson himself asked that the session be held, the governor agreed and called the meeting for August 9th. Carrie Chapman Catt, president of the National American Suffrage Association, and other prominent feminine suffragist leaders hurried to Tennessee to lead the fight. Both presidential candidates, Harding and Cox, had been persistently polled by the women and had eventually declared themselves in favor of the amendment. At the time, however, there was a women's anti-suffragist organization and a men's anti-suffragist union in Tennessee working tirelessly to defeat the amendment. Commented Carrie Chapman Catt:

> Never in the history of politics has there been such a nefarious lobby. . . . They appropriated our telegrams, tapped our telephones, listened outside our windows and transoms. They attacked our private and public lives.

But the legislature met and was urged by the governor to ratify, and the indications were strong that it would do so. The ratification resolution, which required the approval of both houses, was introduced in both on the following day. In the senate, the amendment won handily by a vote of 25 to 4. Not so in the house of representatives. There the speaker, who was in favor of the amendment, changed his mind and voted against it. He claimed that he had also lined up fifty-three other negative votes, more than enough for defeat. The house committee, nevertheless, on August 17th voted to report the measure favorably, and it went before the house as a whole. But before action could be taken, the opposition got through a motion for adjournment. The climax came next day. One legislator, R. L. Dowlen, was ill, but he arose from his bed and went to the capitol to vote for the amendment. Another, T. A. Dodson, had received a message the night before that his baby was dying. He boarded the next train home, and when he left the measure had not yet been called up. His departure left less than a quorum in the house, and as soon as this was discovered by the amendment's backers, they made a rush to catch him. A member in a high-powered car sped to the railroad station, hurriedly obtained a permit to get through the gates to the train, brushed aside the porter, and dashed into the car where Dodson was. The grieving man was told that he must get off the train and come back or the measure would be lost. Dodson hesitated, and the train began to move. Finally he agreed, and the two jumped from the moving train to the platform. Back in the house, Dodson cast his vote — and the result was a tie.

Harry T. Burn, scholarly young representative from McMinn County, East Tennessee, and a neighbor of mine, then on the final ballot decided to vote "aye," and the Nineteenth Amendment was ratified, 49 to 47. He had been in favor of the amendment all the time, Burn told me later, but for some reason was under the impression that most of his constituents opposed it. Said he:

> My mother wanted me to vote for ratification. I appreciated the fact that an opportunity was mine such as seldom comes to mortal man — to free 17,000,000 women from political slavery; I desired that my party, in both state and nation, might say that it was a Republican from the mountains of East Tennessee, the purest Anglo-Saxon section in

the world, who made national Woman's Suffrage possible at this date.

Charges of bribery were made against Burn, but went unproved. Its opponents tried with every trick and parliamentary maneuver they could think of to circumvent the legislation, but they could not. By the single vote of Harry Burn, Tennessee became the thirty-sixth state to ratify the Nineteenth Amendment and make it a part of our Constitution.

VII

Mountain Music

Wᴇʟʟsᴘʀɪɴɢ of the national phenomenon known as "hill-billy music" is the Great Smoky Mountain region. Of course much of it had spilled over into neighboring hills and valleys before it became an accepted jukebox commodity, but its birthplace was the mountain cabin fireside which looked out "On Top of Old Smoky."

Even the name "Tennessee" is a composer's gem. It fits euphoniously into the Tin Pan Alley tunesmith's kit of tools, like the June moon and the love above. Columnist Robert Ruark, in his resentment against the food of honky-tonk cooks, wrote that "it could be that their culinary brains have been battered out by constant repetitions of hillbilly renditions of songs with the word Tennessee in them." Strong words indeed, from a North Carolina native. However that may be, folks from coast to coast continue to be charmed by the melodies of such as *The Tennessee Waltz* and *Carolina in the Morning*.

Since the war, mountain music has reached new heights of popularity from the Pierre in New York to the Palladium in Los Angeles, a popularity that bids fair to remain stable and to provide a new layer in the strata of American music.

A flip of a radio or television dial brings streamlined samples galore, usually with a name singer from New York or Hollywood backed up by a large orchestra rendering extraordinary arrangements of simple hillbilly songs.

There are as many origins of this folk music as there are popular versions. Each song grew in its own Topsy-like way, receiving individual treatment, personal nourishment, and on-the-spot changes. The modern upswing of interest, however, dates roughly from about 1925. Likewise in England, where most of the melodies originated, there has been a considerable effort within the last quarter of a century to collect and preserve the remains of the original country folk music, the cultural tradition of old rural people who are rapidly dying out and taking the songs with them.

The songs of the Southern mountaineers are considered by many authorities to be the only true folk music ever produced by the white men in this country. They have very little connection with Negro folk music, because there are comparatively few Negroes in these mountains, and there were even fewer when the songs were growing up. The music of the mountaineer has a universal flavor all its own, dealing with emotions and truths which are accepted by people whether they are in a metropolis or far from the nearest highway. The melodies are monotonous, and there is a reason: What is repeated is remembered.

When in the eighteenth century the British pioneers pushed into the fastnesses of Tennessee and North Carolina to establish new homes, they brought with them their native ballads — stories of broken faith and parted lovers, the greatest being usually the saddest. Most of these songs were not written down when they first arrived, but the mountain women later "scripted down" some, thus making it easier for modern ballad hunters to collect and identify them. In the ballads there were allusions to kings, lords, and ladies. As time went on and the memory of man ran not far enough backward to be exact, these references to nobles were changed to rivers and mountains, or the lord became a young local swain and the lady his sweetheart, though a few of them, like *Barbara Allen*, the most popular of all, retained their original form.

As the settlers became more Americanized, so did their music. The songs took on new shadings as well as meanings, becoming adjusted to the strange, wild environment of their singers; and as the circumstances and personalities of the newcomers changed, the music kept pace, until it came to interpret, as music always does, the life of a people in all its varied phases. It sang of trials and struggles and of the constant fight with the wilderness. Fun was eclipsed by hardship, death was a more favored theme than birth. The stillness and solitude of the hills and valleys engendered ballads known as "lonesome tunes." Though love is referred to, it is not the maudlin sentiment which runs through Tin Pan Alley ditties. The Smoky Mountaineer's attitude toward the greatest affection has been, and to a great extent still is, one of taking it for granted. It either exists between man and wife, swain and sweetheart, or it doesn't. The most logical cause for its inclusion in a song is its severance or absence. The dread of Indian attack had its counterpart in sad songs. Hunting and fishing found their outlets; I can well remember my mother singing *Shoot the Buffalo*, *The Preacher Went A-Huntin'*, and *Shoot That Turkey Buzzard*.

The English origin of many of the songs is clearly traceable; a few examples may be noted. *The Drunkard's Dream*, for instance, is a modern version of an old English ballad; *The Wreck of Old 97,* although a true narrative of a train disaster, has the same tune as an older European song; and the various versions of *The Prisoner's Song* go back to the Scottish highlands. A few old people still live in the Smoky Mountains who remember the "singin' ballits" given them by their forefathers. Upon proper inducement, ballad collectors have learned, these patriarchs will reluctantly break into ancient song, rendering in untrained and creaky but melodious voices airs which once rang out across Scotland and Ireland, England and Wales. My grandfather, when past ninety, sang some of these, one, I recall, being *I'm a Lonely Pilgrim Here,* a melancholy song which I have never seen written down anywhere.

A high spot in the appraisal of Southern mountain music came in 1915 when the noted English musicologist, Cecil Sharp, visited the Smoky Mountains. His impressions of the people and their music are noteworthy, especially since he was an observer from another land. First of all, he was tremendously taken with the people themselves, their strong character, their individuality, their isolation and its effects upon them and their music. They were sheltered by rugged mountains from the rest of the world, and by this very condition, he concluded, they had retained in all its purity the most lyrical folk music in the world. He found in the beautiful wilderness a region where singing was almost as common as talking. Old people, parents, children, all sang. The peak of social activity was group singing. Sharp found that the Smoky Mountain tunes were not museum pieces in an "animated musical waxworks" but music with a vital, living quality, "tangy as a crab apple, ebullient as hard cider." In nearly every home there was some kind of musical instrument, a fiddle, "gittar," or "banjer." Here was still preserved, the rare gift of ballad making, that superb method of retaining the almost-dead memories of long ago and keeping them attuned to the liveliness of the present. Where in the average European community musical composition was confined to a few elite, here in the Smokies it was the common practice of all, truly a folkway. He was vividly reminded that singing is the one form of expressive art that can be carried on without any previous education or training.

Sharp took down some of the ballads and made them into a collection. One tune he captured from a burly blacksmith who sang while hammering the iron and blowing the bellows, striking a lick, then singing a phrase. In another instance a hint of how ballads are born was given Sharp by a girl who was trying to remember a song: "If I were only driving the cows home, I could sing it for you right away." Another had to go into her home and walk about as if attending to her household chores in order to recall particular songs.

On one occasion, Sharp was puzzled by the expression "ninety girls" in a certain song. A comparison with its English original revealed that the phrase had first been "nightingales," but there being no nightingales in the Smoky Mountains, the words had become meaningless, so "ninety girls" was substituted.

Soon after Sharp's visit, Howard Brockway, an American musical historian born in Brooklyn, visited the Smokies. He wrote:

> We stepped out of New York into the life of the frontier settler of Daniel Boone's time. Here are people who know naught of the advance which has been made in the world outside their mountains. It surpasses belief. In the 17th

century their ancestors brought the songs from Ireland, England, Scotland and Wales, and they have been handed down orally from generation to generation. Songs that died out in the old country a century ago are still sung every day in the Appalachian region. The statement has been made that among these people one can find nearly all the folk songs ever sung in the British Isles.

Although many of the mountain melodies came from beyond the sea, the words which have been later put to them, as well as the variations of the tunes themselves, give them such a distinctly American flavor that they have come to be accepted as domestic products. And they remain continually in the process of change, acquiring new words and twists of tunes according to the individual tastes and experiences of the singers. One note may cover one word on one occasion, and the next time may span a whole phrase. And there may be overtones and suggestions of nature's chorus — the whispering night-sounds of autumn, the dropping of leaves, cries of the wild beasts, war whoops of the Indians, the sweet lonesome songs of the birds, the rush of springs, branches, creeks, rivers.

A favorite time for singing ballads was on the occasion of courting. A young man took his banjo or guitar to his girl's cabin, and there in a straightforward manner, with little change in facial expression and without looking directly at her, he sang out his story of love, often framed as a tale of others but with a meaning clear to his intended. If the ballad did not happen to have words which properly conveyed his meaning, the suitor changed them, and altered the rhythm and melody as required; thus a new ballad was born. On other occasions songs were created when members of a group met at a mountain store or post office, and while sitting around, some whittling, each would improvise a couplet about some local incident — some scandal, accident, or crime. Before the gathering broke up, the one who had the best memory took pride in reciting the whole set of spontaneous verses, and those who had banjos or guitars would pick out on their resonant strings an original tune to accompany it. Those who later repeated these impromptu songs before other gatherings performed the same functions as the medieval balladeers and minnesingers. Fresh in my memory are delightful times at the home of a favorite aunt, when my cousins, brothers, and I sat around the fireplace on winter evenings, making up humorous rhymes and humming them to music.

Ballads about feuding are numerous, but seem somewhat on the decline in popular usage. Feuds have existed in these mountains just as they did between the clans of Scotland, but their importance has been exaggerated by writers and composers who have seized upon the more sensational phases of local life and painted it in extra-lurid tones. In the early days, a "feudin' family" was upheld by relatives and neighbors and described in song. Ballads were composed about the deeds and deaths of the participants, and subsequently picked up by other folks far removed from the scene. Few of their authors are known, since most were the work of several composers, who as time went on modified the original ballad until it became a collective creation.

Generally speaking, the Smoky Mountain ballad is a narrative. It tends frequently to the descriptive and the sad, as the following stanza from a Tennessee work ballad, recalled by Ethel C. Syford of Washington, D.C., reveals:

> Oh the honeysuckle vine
> That's a-windin' 'cross the door,
> An' the rooster chantin' at the break o' day,

An' the bird a-singin' loud,
All are snarkin' at my heart,
An' a-drippin' me with tears o' lonesomeness.

All the early settlers did not remain in these hills. Many of them, especially the shiftless, tarried awhile, then pushed onward. By 1790 almost two hundred thousand persons had poured into the Smoky Mountain Country through the Cumberland Gap, but only a fraction of this number remained. The migration in and out had its effects upon the folk music. The bullwhackers who drove the wagons sang as they went. Those who followed sang of their hard and dangerous lives. Whenever they stopped to rest, music was the accepted diversion. The remains of their travel tunes can be discerned in the songs which have come down from that period, and can be distinguished by their vitality and the power of their rhythm.

The first railroad to pass through East Tennessee began to operate in 1889, and the trains also cast their spell upon the regional music. Anyone who has heard the rhythmic run of the driving locomotive wheels up a grade, or the lonesome strain of the steam whistle, can understand this. Nowadays the loud, mechanical moan of the Diesel engine is a more familiar sound in the Smokies, but the steam engine and its haunting whistle music have been preserved forever in song.

Let it not be thought that all mountain music was melancholy. The people did find time for play, although it was short in comparison to their working hours. There were spells, such as when the crops were laid by, when little physical labor was required, especially outdoors. Then the fiddle became the symbol of fun-making, for its sound meant dancing, and the old fiddle tunes which have come down and lasted were used originally for dancing. Many singing verses of these sprang from the spontaneous words of the dance callers. Their grammatical construction was often awkward and their meaning sometimes vague, for the callers had to fill in between the dances somehow, and, usually blurted out whatever words came first to mind, ad-libbing as best they could. Examples of this music, still popular, are *The Girl I Left behind Me*, originally an old Irish air but adopted by the soldiers of the Confederate Army and later by the U.S. Cavalry, when it was blessed with horses; *Cripple Creek*, a banjo favorite; *Sweet Marie, Old Gray Goose, Cotton-Eyed Joe, Bucking Mule, Cackling Hen, Cornstalk Fiddle, Horse Goes Neigh, Who Bit the Tater?*, and *Old Joe Clark*.

The fiddler used not only his instrument but his whole body, rocking from side to side, smiling and grimacing, patting his foot as if his life depended on it. His fiddle was usually of wood, although in the very early days some were made from cornstalks or gourds. The music he played — always by ear — was as well known to his audience as to him, and the listeners and dancers participated in it with him, swinging and humming and clapping their hands at the proper times. Reels and jigs were the most popular; suited to stringed instruments, they were originally played on the dulcimer, a guitar-like instrument popular for a long time in the mountains. When the fiddlers happened to be stimulated by corn whiskey, they let their imaginations play upon their busy strings, bringing forth figurations surprising even to themselves. Slow melodies grew dramatic and rhythm increased in dynamic quality; new tunes grew out of old.

Some of the mountain people danced, others felt that pastime was the work of the Devil. But parents who objected to dancing would permit their daughters to play musical games;

and from this grew the "play party," held in the front yard, or on any kind of ground, by the light of candles, lanterns, or just the moon. The music was furnished by the players themselves, and was entirely vocal. This form of amusement was to the summer evenings what the literary society, which flourished at the same time, was to the winter. To both came not only the young people but the old as well; and while the former played, their elders talked and watched, and the younger children slept.

At times it was hard to tell the difference between play parties and dances, but there was just enough difference to allay the consciences of the most religious. Musical numbers frequently used were *Here Come Three Dukes, The Miller Boy, Old Dan Tucker, Weevily Wheat,* and *Skip to My Lou,* the last-named being pronounced so fast that for years I thought it was all one word. The varying of musical themes and changing of partners were the chief elements of the play party. In *The Miller Boy,* for instance, men and girls formed couples and marched about in a circle, while one girl remained alone outside the ring and in the middle stood a man without a partner. When the word "grab" was spoken — which might come any time the music stopped — the pairs uncoupled, the man in the middle tried to obtain a partner, and the girl on the outside entered the general scramble. Instantly a new ring would be formed, separating the slowest couple from each other as before. During these musical games, heads and elbows moved up and down but that was about all; the partners never touched each other except with hands, arms, or shoulders. In *Old Dan Tucker* the girls lined up facing the men. At the singing of the second stanza, the first man pursued the first girl down between the two files and back up on the outside. If he caught her before she reached her place at the head of the line, he was permitted to kiss her, usually amid gently protesting squeals from her and general teasing from the group.

A highlight in the musical life of a community was a "working." For this event, invitations were sent to everyone within miles around. Guests came early and, unless they had an automobile, as in later times, stayed until they could return home by daylight. Beds and other furniture were removed from the front room of the house. The women started off the singing and dancing festivities, while the men stood around outside waiting their turn to join in the fun. These parties were held in connection with new ground clearings, house raisings, corn shuckings, apple peelings, molasses stir-offs, and quiltings. Some of the songs were preserved by the young ladies, who often on Sunday afternoons following the parties would write them down in scrapbooks which they hid away in their attics.

The White Spirituals

Extremely important to the people of the Smoky Mountains are their religious songs. These have a history of their own. Their origins are somewhat haphazard, but the songs themselves are more homogeneous than the social folk songs. They are often monotonously repetitious, which has a decided effect upon the rural congregations, resulting in weeping and even shouting. Little dialect is found in them, probably because most are the compositions of ministers who traveled more than their fellow-composers of the secular world, and thus acquired better education and less mountain mannerisms of speech. Finally, the white spirituals must not be confused with those of the Negroes. There is a similarity, but the Negro spirituals have different origins, mainly in the deep South.

Though the religious songs passed over denominational lines, the question did arise on at least one occasion. Ethel Park Richardson, the writer and song compiler, noted that in the spiritual *Don't You Hear Jerusalem Moan?* there was a long listing of denominations which, however, excepted the Episcopalians.

"Aren't there any Episcopalians in these mountains?" she asked one woman.

"I don't know if there is," was the slow reply. "Jed has kilt about every kind of varmint there is in these mountains. Ef there is any of them you jist mentioned, you'll find hits hide in the shed out there."

The great religious revival which swept the southern Appalachians in the beginning of the nineteenth century, left its imprint on East Tennessee's music. This was the day of the camp meeting, and the revival reached a climax in a series of these fervent gatherings which, taken together, were known as the Great Revival. Evangelists, disregarding denominational lines, held a preaching marathon. The people stopped work, loaded their families into the crude wagons or walked them down the trails, and stayed for weeks at picturesque campgrounds such as Carpenter's, which looks across at the magnificent forms of the bright-blue Smokies. Tents, covered wagons, and hastily built cabins sheltered the vast crowds. Night and day the fiery evangelists exhorted their flocks, like Moses and the Prophets, to refrain from pride, fashion, vanity, jesting, swearing, drunkenness, fornication, gambling, dancing, malice, revenge, and worldliness.

What was one of these meetings like? It was usually held on a plot of ground as large as a football field, often surrounded by trees. The gathering time was dusk, and the flickering light of campfires threw grotesque shadows upon the figures of the milling people. Bearded men in the stern dress of the day passed to and fro, taking their women to places on the split logs used for seats. The men's hair was long and roughly bobbed just above their collars; their homemade trousers fit tightly, as did their coats. The women wore dark, stiff bonnets which almost hid their faces. Although there was much movement, the sounds were muffled and reverent, those who spoke doing so in low tones. Up front a white-bearded patriarch arose and without ado started a hymn. At first he read it aloud, speaking the lines in a sonorous, sepulchral voice. Then the congregation joined in, and the whole landscape resounded with the full consonance of their voices. As the darkness grew deeper, the words of the preacher became more exhorting, his tales of hellfire more crackling. Another hymn was sung, and in its measures an emotional crescendo was reached, with sobs and shouts now interspersing its solemn strains. As if impelled, some of the audience arose and made their way to the front to kneel down and ask for mercy. Others searched for friends in order to lead them to the altar to be saved. A sinner who felt redemption suddenly rose to his feet, and shouts of joy went up from all over the huge throng. More saved sinners followed; some laughed, shouted, and fainted away, others became convulsed, their heads jerking back and forth with remarkable rapidity. On and on went the sermon into the late hours, until at length the final song and benediction came. The exhausted people stood in mute reverence while the old minister prayed, actually delivering a sermon in miniature but this one spoken in the direction of the Lord. At last the silence was broken by low words and the sound of departing wagons, as the lights of the campground were finally extinguished and the people faded away into the night.

L. L. McDowell and George Pullen Jackson regard these camp meetings as the source of many of the extant white spirituals. Some of the songs were composed by the preachers who led them, often utilizing words and snatches of melody picked up from previous meetings. They were sung in unison, and the verses were repeated until a frenzy resulted, the impassioned singers doubling and trebling the last stanzas in fervor and volume. Getting off key made little difference. Most of the songs were sung from memory, in the natural, untrained way of enthusiastic singers who could not have read notes had they been written down. Two typical songs that were born of the great camp meetings, *I'm a Lonely Pilgrim Here* and *Let's Go Down in the Valley to Pray*, have a beauty poignant and moving.

Reminiscent of those camp-meeting days are the groups of Old Harp Singers which exist in the Smoky Mountain Country. The name is derived from the songbook they use, first published in Knoxville in 1849 and originally called *The Harp of Columbia,* later *The New Harp of Columbia* compiled by W. H. and M. L. Swan. It employs a curious musical notation — the notes appear on the staff in the proper position, but may also instantly be recognized by their individual shape, each having a different contour.

Although he died at the age of thirty-two, M. L. Swan led an active and unusual life. Born in Alabama, he was afflicted with rheumatism from an early age. He served in the Confederate Army but saw no action because of his ailment. After the war he began to teach singing schools in East Tennessee, and at the time of his premature death had made $75,000 from this work. He was devoted to music even to the point of absent-mindedness. One day in Chattanooga he chanced upon a big man wearing a suit with large, loud checks. Swan was impressed with the similarity of the suit's pattern to the staff lines and "shape notes" of printed songs, and without a thought drew close to the man and began pointing out "notes" on his coat and singing "do, re, mi." The owner of the garment was so insulted that he jerked it off and threw it on the ground preparatory to giving Swan a threshing. The latter, however, still dreamily fascinated by the coat, calmly walked over to where it lay, got down on his knees beside it, and continued singing. In disbelief and disgust the big fellow snatched up the coat and snorted. "Well, if he's such a danged, crazy fool, I jist caint whup him!"

Some flavor of the old camp meetings with their white spirituals can be recaptured each year at the world meeting of the Church of God in Cleveland, Tennessee. One such was attended a few years ago by this writer. Inside the big tabernacle where the convention was held, a huge choir stood on the stage, containing mostly singers but also a few guitar and violin players. Outside a great crowd of those who could not get in milled about. Every hotel and tourist camp in the city was filled with the visitors, as well as every private home that would accommodate them. Some delegates even had to sleep in the open streets.

The Heyday of Hillbilly Tunes

In the years since the beginning of the century, many changes have been wrought in the Smoky Mountain way of life, but there has been less change in its hillbilly music than one might think. It has been dressed up; it is on millions of records, on the radio, in the movies, on television; the trees and hills which furnished its early background have given way to the streamlined studio; and its musicians dress according to the Broadway or Hollywood version of hill folks, rather than naturally. But it's still the same old music.

During the Depression, when most of the nation was blighted by economic failures, the Smoky Mountain Country was aided by the inauguration of the Tennessee Valley Authority. The entry of this modern phenomenon into the sylvan scene revolutionized the lives of the people, and the most touching phase of the upheaval was the uprooting of family homesteads which had stood for generations, in order to clear the land for the dams and lakes of TVA. Typical of the songs which sprang out of the anxious hearts of these displaced people was the following, written by Cleatus Burnett of Sharps Chapel, Tennessee, who fitted the words to the tune of *Red River Valley*.

> *When the old Cove Creek Dam*
> *First was started, most everyone*
> *Said it would be so grand,*
> *For they did not realize*
> *Water was going to cover the land.*
>
> *So goodbye to old Union County,*
> *It's the dear, sweet home of my birth.*
> *There's no other place before her,*
> *She's the sweetest place on this earth.*

Modern-style troubadours such as Bascom Lunsford, Jim Garland, Sarie Ogan, and Aunt Mollie Jackson sang of the new days in the mountains, of the good old days and the bad years which followed, of the WPA and the TVA, of long-gone lovers and new heroes. In the towns on Saturday afternoons, crowds of country people gathered in furniture stores, milled into the phonograph booths, and listened to the recorded songs of their favorites, including Jimmie Rogers, the Carter Family, Uncle Dave Macon, DeFord Bailey, and other string-and-voice experts. Sometimes these "customers" bought a recording, usually they just listened and then perfunctorily went their way — often into the next furniture store.

As the Second World War approached, the music of the Southern highlands was getting around more and more. Those who had felt that the "mountain intonation" was nothing but an unpleasant kind of "yodel by yokels" were coming to recognize in the nasal inflections a charm and natural color. The general result was that the music molded by the experiences of our early past was kept alive, active and useful. Big-time dance orchestras parodied the hillbilly songs, yet they could hardly improve on the raw humor that came out of the mountains in such songs as the following:

> *I've been a moonshiner*
> *For seventeen long years.*
> *I've spent all my money*
> *On whiskey and beers.*
> *I'll go to some holler*
> *And put up my still.*
> *I'll sell you one gallon*
> *For a two-dollar bill.*

By 1949 hillbilly music, according to *Down Beat* magazine, was pushing popular tunes, jazz, bebop, and such out of the musical limelight. Where once a hillbilly recording sold ten thousand copies, it was now selling close to fifty. No longer were the sales confined to the South; they had reached national and international proportions. Radio stations from

Savannah to New York City played the mountain music for as much as eighteen hours a day. City slickers learned to square dance, and night clubs were turned into log-cabin reproductions for atmosphere.

The war had done a lot to spread hillbilly tunes. Most of the large military training camps were in the South, some in the shadows of the Great Smokies, and GI's from the North who had never heard this music now heard it constantly — and liked it. When they went home, they took along recordings, and their families joined the hillbilly trend. The country seemed to want simpler songs — and got them in these upland tunes. Shifts in population led by defense workers from the South who went North, taking their native music along with them, helped spread the craze; then came the disc jockeys. Jo Stafford, who has a peculiarly appropriate voice with a rich, high timbre, recorded her famous hick version of the sophisticated dance song *Temptation,* and Dinah Shore, a native Tennessean, changed the European waltz *Forever and Ever* into a hillbilly hit. *Good Night, Irene* gave the whole nation a musical urge to retire, and *The Tennessee Waltz* capped them all with an unprecedented five-million recordings sold in a little over a year.

To the center of the rustic song stage stepped Eddie Arnold of Henderson, Tennessee, who went from a plowboy to rank with Perry Como as a popular singer. When Arnold was seven years old, his family gave him an old Sears, Roebuck guitar on which he promptly took four lessons at seventy-five cents each. Immediately thereafter he started out playing chords at Saturday night hoedown dances, then got on Station WSM in Nashville, where he had a six-days-a-week program playing and singing. By 1944 RCA had signed him up, and within three years his drawling baritone recordings of *I'll Hold You in My Heart, Bouquet of Roses,* and the ancient *Molly Darling* were leading the weekly national folk-song jukebox polls. Arnold appeared on the "Grand Ole Opry" radio program from Nashville, made a movie entitled *Hoedown* for $250,000, and toured the United States making personal appearances at $5000 a night. Later he went into television. He is the more conventional type of hillbilly singer, and his selections run less to the original mountain type than those of some others. Asked if he had really been a plowboy, Arnold said: "Boy, I sure did plow. That's why I wanted to learn to play that guitar and sing so I wouldn't have to keep plowin' all my life."

Called "the King" by his friends and not disposed to deny it is Roy Acuff, foremost modern exponent of mountain music. He has become not only a national musical figure with a fabulous income, but for a time attracted countrywide attention as a political campaigner and possible governor of the state. Roy Acuff grew up in the Smoky Mountains, where his father was a Baptist preacher in the area near Knoxville. Roy never took a music lesson in his life, and those who don't care for his type of music regard this fact as obvious. But folks in Tennessee tell a story to the effect that at the peak of the fighting on Okinawa, a Jap banzai charge on a Marine position was accompanied by yells of "To hell with President Roosevelt! To hell with Roy Acuff!"

This most famous of the hillbilly singers makes over $200,000 a year from fiddling, leading a string band, making personal appearances and movies. He stated that his song *Wabash Cannonball* grossed $5,000,000 at seventy-nine cents a recording, and that another, *Precious Jewel,* sold almost as well. The former song is an old one, but Roy added a realistic railroad whistle said to be most authentic, which he learned to execute while working as a callboy for the Louisville & Nashville Railroad. Roy's first ambition was to play baseball. He pitched for Knoxville Central High School and became so good that the New York Yankees offered him a tryout. But while he was in Florida getting ready for his big chance, he suffered a sunstroke which laid him up so long it destroyed his baseball ambitions. While convalescing at his home in Tennessee, his "ma" bought him a secondhand fiddle. In the house also were an old phonograph and a number of mountain-music records. With time to listen to them over and over again, Roy learned the tunes by heart and then picked them out on his fiddle. But he knew more about the songs than just their music. He was part of their background. On a tenant farm at the edge of the Smokies, he had followed a mule and plow between the corn rows and had also broken his share of new ground. His fun had come at such events as corn shuckings, where a jug of moonshine was hidden in the middle of the pile and the contestants shucked to see who could get to it first. Of course there was music on these occasions, and Roy Acuff became saturated with the natural melodious atmosphere of his native country.

After he had recovered from his two-year convalescence, Roy spent the next three trying to get into radio. The station executives wanted him to croon, but he could not. He begged them to let him sing just as he had back in the mountains. Finally they gave in, and Roy gave out with an offering entitled *The Great Speckled Bird*. The audience loved it, and he was made. He became a regular performer on the NBC Grand Ole Opry show from Nashville, and from that moment on his fame took leaps and bounds. During the next twenty years his recordings sold more than twenty-five million copies. In the European Theater during the Second World War, he was voted more popular than Frank Sinatra.

True to his mountain traditions, Roy's favorite songs are those about love not attained, hearts breaking, people dying. Though hillbilly acts are normally humorous, when he sings the humor is put aside. As the introduction is played, Roy drops his head in a prayerful attitude, then throws it back, looks up toward the sky, and lets loose. His voice actually becomes choked up, and tears run down his cheeks. His sincere belief in what he sings has brought him requests to become a preacher. In Constitution Hall in Washington he once played to a capacity crowd that had paid as much as $6.60 apiece to hear him. On a pier at Venice, California, twenty thousand people swarmed to see and hear him, until it was feared the pier would fall under the weight. Roy owns a music publishing house in Nashville, a $200,000 resort near there, a swimming pool, a dance hall, and a one hundred-room hotel. His hobby is collecting hand-painted neckties, and he has also gathered unto himself over a thousand miniature liquor bottles.

In 1948 Roy decided to run for governor of Tennessee on the Republican ticket, after his friends had kidded him so much about it that he determined to "show 'em." He was duly nominated, and had as his running mate for senator a wealthy banker and longtime congressman from the First District, B. Carroll Reece, former Republican national chairman. The two contrasting candidates put on a rollicking campaign built around "Roy Acuff and His Smoky Mountain Boys," a top-notch hillbilly aggregation. But though they attracted the largest crowds in the state's political history, Reece and Acuff lost to Estes Kefauver and Gordon Browning. The experience, instead of diminishing Roy's musical success, increased it. Asked how he had done so well in his field, he replied: "Everything I am has growed up with me. It's the kind of people we are."

Grand Ole Opry

The vehicle which has done most to spread mountain music across the country is the Grand Ole Opry radio show, heard every Saturday night in the year from Nashville over the full National Broadcasting Company network. It is the oldest and longest show in radio, plays to the nation's largest studio audience, and is regularly listened to by an estimated ten million persons.

Grand Ole Opry was born in 1925 when a seventy-year-old fiddler named Uncle Jimmy Thompson dropped into WSM's studios in Nashville and offered to play on the air. The announcer, George Dewey Hay, later to become known as the "Solemn Old Judge," put him in front of the microphone and let him loose. An hour later, Uncle Jimmy was asked if he weren't tired.

"Tired!" he snorted. "Heck, I'm only gettin' started. I played all night last night at a fair."

The response to this experiment was enthusiastic. Listeners wanted more of Uncle Jimmy and his like. The Grand Ole Opry was the result. Soon a string band, organized by a country doctor named Humphrey Bate, played on the show; it was named the Possum Hunters, and was followed by the Gully Jumpers, the Fruit Jar Drinkers, and the Crook Brothers. The name of the program itself grew out of an announcement which Walter Damrosch made on the air, concerning realism in grand opera. Just as the famous conductor signed off in his appealing way, the Solemn Old Judge came on from WSM with this explanation: "From here on, folks, it will be nothing but realism of the realest kind. You've just been up in the air with grand opera. Now get down to earth with us in a performance of *Grand Ole Opry!*"

The four-hour show began to attract not only the barn-dance crowd but also those who had migrated to the cities and ardently wanted to retain contact with their rural homes. A measure of its popularity was the growth of its studio audience. At first only one hundred fifty persons squeezed into the Opry studio. Later it was enlarged to accommodate five hundred, but even with this capacity the manager had to put the show on in two shifts to take care of the crowds. Officials of the National Life and Accident Insurance Company, which owns the radio station, tried to enter the company building at 9:30 one Saturday night for an emergency meeting. They found five hundred devoted fans waiting outside for the Grand Ole Opry to begin. When the officials tried to enter, their ears were assailed with shouts of "Oh no you don't!" and "Git to the end of the line!" Next day, the Opry was told to move its audiences elsewhere. It tried a small movie theater, then a former tabernacle, but all proved too small. Finally the Opry moved to its present location, the Ryman Auditorium in Nashville, where five thousand persons somehow squeeze into thirty-seven hundred seats each Saturday night "as raglar as bathin' time." Tickets are sold out a month ahead, and there's always a waiting line for last-minute vacancies.

Venerable star of the show is Uncle Dave Macon, eighty-five years old at this writing, who for thirty-six years was "conductor of a double-shovel plow." But his hobby was the "banjer," and it led him into the Grand Ole Opry, fame, and fortune from his Tennessee-country-ham-growing farm at appropriately named Readyville. Red Foley, the singing master of ceremonies, whose recordings at times outsell those of Bing Crosby, is becoming a leading figure in the field of American folk music. He has a rich, sweet voice that is equally at home with a hoedown or spiritual. Roy Acuff and his Smoky Mountain Boys returned to the show after their popularity took a dip during an absence from it. Rod Brasfield is the leading comedian, with a sort of corny, Will Rogers style, and Cousin Minnie Pearl, "The Girl from Grinder's Switch," plays the hillbilly girl. In all, about one hundred twenty-five entertainers appear on the Opry each Saturday night during its full run of four hours, the main half-hour of which is sponsored by the R. J. Reynolds Tobacco Company.

Besides the millions who hear it on the air, the Opry has brought an estimated five million visitors to Nashville in the past quarter of a century. More important is its great influence in emphasizing the place American folk music has in our lives, thus helping it to survive and grow. From Cracklin' Creek to Carnegie Hall, this symbolic radio show has captured the musical heart of the nation. For it is more than a radio show: it is the glorification of all the simple home-musical shindigs that have been taken part in by so many average people, who still hold the memories close to their hearts.

VIII

The Monkey Trial

On the hot and drowsy afternoon of July 20, 1925, in the usually tranquil town of Dayton near the Smokies, a strange drama was taking place. In the center of a typical courthouse lawn, near the torrid bricks of the old building itself, the climax of a mighty legal struggle was approaching. The two principal contestants were William Jennings Bryan and Clarence Darrow; their goal, ostensibly the guilt or innocence of a Dayton high-school teacher named John Thomas Scopes, actually the refutation or corroboration of Charles Darwin. For Bryan, it was appropriately the seventh day of the trial. Around the two men, spread out in sweating profusion, were their immediate supporters, forming a small nucleus of a vast audience throughout the world which by means of telegraph and the printed page was following the blow-by-blow account with fascinated attention.

If the only issue had been a clash between two great reputations or even between the principles of religion and science, the spectacle would have been less momentous, particularly for the people of the region. But this was more than a glorified trial. It was also a carnival of cranks, a rendezvous of the ridiculous. To unassuming little Dayton, with its average citizens typical of the mountain country, had come a motley multitude of freakish people from all parts of the country. The turnout for the event was a combination of a mammoth county fair and the Coney Island Midway. One venerable resident described the scene as resembling "a livery stable." From the courthouse, as far as the eye could see, people were massed in striking confusion. The main street beside the square was filled for blocks with standees, like the rear of a popular theater. In the alleys that stretched away from the street, scores of lunchstands and other concessions had been set up end to end, with operators loudly hawking their wares. All the hotels were filled to the brim, their hallways jammed with cots, some visitors even sleeping on the hot roofs. There was not a home in Dayton with a few square feet of space to spare that did not accommodate one or more out-of-towners. No greater claim to fame exists in the town today than the proud statements of two old families that "Darrow stayed at our house" and "Bryan slept here."

As if the daytime excitement and confusion during the trial proceedings were not enough, the carnival carried on at night. This was indeed when the rasher spirits among those on hand came out like witches and brewed their stormy cups of dissension. Never has there been assembled in this country a greater variety of atheists, quacks, cranks, fanatics, and cultural hoodlums than was present at the Scopes Trial. They swarmed into town like camp followers at a military bivouac. During the day their attention was focused on the trial itself, but when dusk began to creep over the valley they put on their little individual shows of speeches and harangues for the benefit of anyone who would show interest and many who would not. Communists, Socialists, Anarchists, all foregathered, and many a real soapbox was utilized in true Union Square style. The radicals vied with the atheists in trying to catch the public eye and ear, while muttering groups of young natives looked threateningly on. Through each night these visiting oddities held forth, using the electric street lights as long as they were on, then plying their oratory by the weird glow of wooden torches cut from nearby trees. They had lost no time in rushing to Dayton to jump on the bright bandwagon, and they lost no time during the trial, making every lull in the main proceedings count in their program of vilification of religion and government. If some of the local people identified this riffraff as the followers, even cohorts, of Darrow and the other defense attorneys as well as the "sophisticated" writers present, they could hardly be blamed, so dramatically did the soapboxers acquit themselves on the sidelines. The pamphlets they handed out and left behind after they had gone did nothing, either, to relieve the impression that an array of Philistines had descended from the North, and were fortunate indeed not to have been smitten by the sword of the Almighty.

Some of the main actors in the great drama fared little better in the opinion of those who were termed "hill billies" by visiting journalists. No dirt farmer of the region, with one suspender, sweaty shirt, and mouthful of frequently-squirted tobacco, looked any homelier than Clarence Darrow. Bainbridge Colby, Wilson's Secretary of State, was there for the defense, looking like "something out of a Fifth Avenue tailor shop, with straight, black clothes, ram-rod posture, and a handsome, dark mustache which seemed to prevent its owner from going into any place that even smacked of the improper."

The press had a field day. From far and near newspapermen had come to cover the event, exhorted by their editors that here was a headline fiesta, and anything less than screaming banner-lines on the front page would be disappointing news indeed. The wire services had set up a special message-sending headquarters near the courthouse, and daily flooded the country and world with telegraphic reports until the volume of verbiage sent out was, according to Bryan, "greater than for any other event up to that time, except the World War." One reporter became overzealous as to the final decision of Judge John T. Raulston, filed a premature story that Scopes had been adjudged guilty — and quickly found himself held in contempt of court. With ox-tongue in cheek, H. L. Mencken penned clever words for his eastern readers about the "yokels" of the region who watched in open-mouthed wonder the activities of "civilized persons" for the first time. He named the region "the Bible Belt," a compliment which the residents, as a whole, accepted gratefully and are proud of to this day. (Other, less tolerant natives didn't like Mencken's fiery ridicule, and passed the word along not too quietly that "this pole cat had better get out of town while he's able.") H. K. Hollister, a writer-photographer, ran about with one of the newfangled movie cameras, taking pictures of the main event and occasionally getting in some shots of the crowd, many of which outran him in an effort to get in front of the camera.

The Tennessee attorneys participating in the trial were, of course, overshadowed by the visiting legal celebrities, although they acquitted themselves well enough when they got a chance to say anything. For the prosecution were Bryan and his son, William Jennings Bryan, Jr.; the local Attorney General (later Senator) A. T. Stewart; B. G. McKenzie and his son, J. G. McKenzie; H. E. Hicks and Sue K. Hicks; and

W. C. Haggard. (Mrs. Ruth Bryan Rohde, Bryan's daughter, told the writer that W. J. Bryan, Jr., took no active part in the trial.) The defense counsel included Clarence Darrow, Bainbridge Colby, Dudley Field Malone, Arthur Garfield Hays, and J. R. Thompson, all from the North; and two local men, John L. Godsey and that perennial office-seeker and liberal, John R. Neal.

An example of Dayton opinion was given me by the late Walter White, superintendent of the Rhea County Schools. He observed:

> Darrow walked like a cat, was not an orator but did have great reasoning powers. Bryan had not been in court for twenty-nine years and could hardly have been expected to outshine the veteran trial lawyer from Chicago, who was fresh from victory in the famous Loeb-Leopold case. However, Bryan did save Darrow from being jailed for contempt of court when the latter overstepped the bounds of proper courtroom procedure and became too sarcastic about one of the judge's decisions.

Although most accounts of the Dayton trial seem to portray it as a struggle between enlightenment and an assortment of ignorant hillbillies whose innate prejudices blinded them, each succeeding year of the quarter-century that has passed since the event has served to refute this notion. There was a social and spiritual significance to the trial which has been perpetuated both in the minds and in the institutions of the South.

The Great Commoner both started and ended it. On January 29, 1925, Bryan made a speech in Nashville on the subject "Is the Bible True?" In the very next session of the state legislature, Representative John Washington Butler of Macon County, a substantial farmer who had read both the Bible and

Darwin's *Origin of Species* and who could not reconcile man's evolution from a lower animal with the book of *Genesis*, introduced a bill which stated:

> . . . that it shall be unlawful for any teacher in any of the Universities, Normals and all other public schools of the State which are supported in whole or in part by the public school funds of the State, to teach any theory that denies the story of the Divine Creation of man as taught in the Bible, and to teach instead that man has descended from a lower order of animals.

This bill became law on March 21st, and although there were many Tennesseans who felt it to be extreme and unnecessary, nevertheless progressive Governor Austin Peay signed it, believing that it would become a dead letter, like so many peculiar laws of other states. But this was not to be.

The law began to attract attention. Some individuals in Chattanooga talked of bringing a test case, but they were too slow. One day in nearby Dayton, at the drugstore of one of the town's leading citizens, F. E. Robinson, a group of men were sitting around a table drinking Coca-Colas, when one of their number, John Thomas Scopes of the high school faculty, remarked that he was using in his science classes a state-adopted textbook, *Hunter's Biology,* which supported the theory of evolution. Scopes said he knew that the state had passed a law prohibiting such teaching, yet the textbook had been passed upon and approved by the state textbook commission. Another member of the group, Dr. George Rapplyea, a local industrialist who also had the makings of a great press agent, slyly suggested that Scopes be arrested for violating the state law. At first the whole thing seemed to be a joke, but the plot thickened, Rapplyea himself swore out a warrant against Scopes — who had been promised that he would suffer no real penalty — and Constable Perry Swafford served the warrant on him right then and there. Then a telephone call was made to the Nashville *Banner,* whose alert editor saw the possibilities of a big scoop and immediately filed a wire story which made headlines throughout the country — and Dayton the cynosure of all eyes.

This may seem to have been merely a publicity stunt. But it was more. The men who were active in bringing about a test of the anti-evolution law, aside from any impulse to pull off a stunt, sincerely believed in the general principles underlying the law itself. With the exception of Scopes, they were representative of the citizens of Dayton and of the Smoky Mountain Country. What many who have recorded their impressions of the trial and its origin seem to have missed is that the people of the section, through every step of the great event and afterward, held firmly to their predominant belief in their oldtime religion. They avowed that if they had to choose between education and religion, or between anything else and religion, they would choose religion. Even Mencken wrote about Tennessee:

> The State, to a degree that should be gratifying, has escaped the national standardization. Its people show a character that is immensely different from the character of, say New Yorkers or Californians. They retain, among other things, the anthropomorphic religion of an elder day. They do not profess it; they believe in it.

With the approach of the trial, these people began to bestir themselves. There was hardly a family which did not have among its prized possessions a well-worn Bible which most of them had read "from kiver to kiver." They saw a challenge, not so much to some details of the Good Book, but to their religion as a whole, something more divinely dear to them than life itself. True, the beginning of life was important; but the ending of life and the eternity beyond were vastly more important. Anyone, they reasoned, who questioned God's creation of man also questioned God's heaven awaiting men who followed His teachings. This was more than a friendly argument between a Methodist and Baptist over the relative merits of sprinkling and immersion. This was a challenge which, they believed, struck at the very foundation of all Christian religion.

From New York City the American Civil Liberties Union offered its services in behalf of Scopes, and engaged Arthur Garfield Hays as one of the counsel for the defense. Scopes, who by this time was beginning to feel embarrassed, was asked to come to New York. While in the metropolis, he was interviewed by the big newspapers, whose articles pointed him up as a modest and sincere person being victimized by the "backward people" of Tennessee. Dudley Field Malone also joined the ranks of the defense. Then Bryan, sensing that his speeches had helped bring on the trial, announced that he would volunteer his services for the prosecution. And in Chicago, his fame recently enhanced by the sensational murder trial of Loeb and Leopold, Clarence Darrow was persuaded by the editor of a local newspaper to enter the forthcoming fray as chief defense counsel. With the announcement of his participation, the public began to realize that this was to be an epochal match between giants, rather than simply the trial of a high-school teacher for violating a state law.

On Friday, July 10, Dayton's Judge John T. Raulston opened court. The weather was the hottest that venerable Dayton citizens could recall, and the judge began by shedding his coat, an example which was followed thankfully by the attorneys. With each succeeding day the crowds grew greater, until toward the end of the trial. Raulston became afraid that the wooden floor of the old courthouse would give way under their weight, and adjourned the proceedings to the lawn outside.

According to custom, the trial was opened with a prayer, which immediately brought a violent objection from Darrow and a heated argument between him and Attorney General A. T. Stewart. This immediately set the tone of the trial, which was to be a series of clashes between opposing counsel over religion and science rather than over the guilt or innocence of Scopes. Arthur Garfield Hays offered a petition that if prayers in the court were necessary, they should be given by ministers of all faiths rather than by Protestants only. Judge Raulston settled this dispute by referring the matter to the Rhea County Pastors' Association, which, to the surprise of the defense counsel, selected a visiting Unitarian minister, Reverend Charles Francis Potter of New York, to give the next prayer. But Darrow insisted that his objection be inserted in the court record each morning, along with the ruling of the judge on it.

Even if the trial's importance did not hinge upon its legal side, the formalities were for the most part observed. The defense moved to quash the indictment of Scopes, claiming it to be in conflict with the constitution of the State of Tennessee and with the Fourteenth Amendment of the Constitution of the United States. This motion was, of course, overruled by the judge, who gave his opinion that the law was valid. Then the defense, led by Darrow, tried a brilliant coup — which failed. This was a strong effort to introduce as expert witnesses a group of eminent scientists who were to testify that modern scientific teaching could not be carried on without acceptance of the theory of evolution. Bryan countered by arguing that such men would only give their own opinions, and asked, if they were admitted, that he be allowed to call in "experts" on religion as well. A prolonged argument ensued over this vital part of the defense plan. After deliberation, Judge Raulston denied the use of expert testimony, but did permit the defense to enter the prepared testimony of the experts in the record.

The people of Tennessee and the South did not lose sight of the brilliance of Darrow. At first outwardly hostile to him, they grew to admire the astuteness of this canny lawyer, even though they differed violently with him on principle. As usual, Darrow fitted adroitly into the local setting, wearing suspenders and a blue shirt, with his loose clothes hanging unkemptly upon his big frame. The consensus of local opinion was fairly summed up in the words of Attorney General Stewart. Said he:

> His courtesy is noticeable — his ability is known — and it is a shame in my mind, in the sight of God, that a mentality like his has strayed so far from the natural goal that it should follow. Great God, the good that a man of his ability could have done if he had aligned himself with the forces of right instead of aligning himself with that which strikes its poisonous fangs at the very bosom of Christianity.

Darrow was not so courteous toward the decision of the judge against admission of expert testimony. In fact, he became so sarcastic about it that Raulston rebuked him sharply and threatened him with discipline, finally citing him for contempt and placing his bail at $5000. At this point Bryan displayed a typical virtue. He went to the judge and interceded in behalf of Darrow, asking that the chief defense attorney be allowed to continue in the trial. Darrow made a fervent apology, and was accordingly freed of the contempt charge.

The vertex of the trial came on its tenth day, when Darrow took the most unusual step in the history of American court proceedings. He called William Jennings Bryan, chief of the prosecution attorneys, to the witness stand. This was with Bryan's permission, however, and the Commoner understood that if he testified under such unorthodox circumstances, he in turn would get a chance to put Darrow on the stand and question him. But because of the peculiar circumstances of the trial, this opportunity never came.

Here then was the *pièce de résistance*, the limelighted climax which the press and public had been waiting for — the central clash between Darrow and Bryan. At this "Monkey Trial," they asked, would Darrow make a monkey out of Bryan? Before the eyes and ears of the fascinated spectators and the busy typewriters of the press, as well as some of radio's first public microphones, the main event unfolded. No Hollywood director could have staged a more dramatic scene. The azure sky, the gentle breeze which quietly fanned the branches of the tall trees in the courtyard, stood in contrast to the tense, heated scene below where two men who had reached the heights of their respective professions crossed swords in a humble seat of American justice.

In a characteristic pose, Darrow stood leaning against a table, in one hand a Bible, in the other a fold of his suspenders which he pushed back and forth nonchalantly, belying in all his motions and in his quiet voice that bright fire which shot from his rapier-like words. Seated opposite him, his countenance serene and confident, Bryan seemed to his many followers the epitome of the eloquent spirit which in earlier days had electrified the country by denouncing its crucifixion on a cross of gold. He had come now to bear another cross.

Darrow: "Do you claim that everything in the Bible should be literally interpreted?"

Bryan: "I believe everything in the Bible should be accepted as it is given there."

Darrow: "When you read that Jonah swallowed the whale — or that the whale swallowed Jonah — excuse me please — how do you literally interpret that?"

Bryan: "It is hard to believe, for you, but easy for me. Let me add: one miracle is just as easy to believe as another."

Darrow: "Perfectly easy to believe that Jonah swallowed the whale?"

Bryan: "If the Bible said so; the Bible doesn't make as extreme statements as Evolutionists do." (Laughter)

Darrow: "Could you come anywhere near how old the earth is?"

Bryan: "I wouldn't attempt to. I could possibly come as near as the scientists do, but I had rather be more accurate before I give a guess." (Laughter)

Darrow: "Do you believe that Joshua made the sun stand still, or that in order to lengthen the day it would have been construed that the earth stood still?"

Bryan (lifting a glass of water from the table): "I would not attempt to say what would have been necessary, but I know this, that I can take a glass of water that would fall to the ground without the strength of my hand, and I can overcome the law of gravitation and lift it up. If my puny hand can overcome the law of gravitation to that extent, I would not deny power to the hand of Almighty God that made the Universe."

As the questioning went on, the repartee of the two men

became more acrid. For two hours, in the furnace-like heat, Darrow assailed Bryan with more than three hundred questions. As they neared the end of the furious exchange of words, their tempers grew short.

Darrow: "Where have you lived all your life?"

Bryan: "Not near you."

Darrow: "Not near anybody of learning."

Bryan: "Oh don't assume you know it all."

The questions descended into name calling. Finally Bryan arose and addressed the judge: "Your Honor, I think I can shorten this testimony. The only purpose Mr. Darrow has is to slur at the Bible. But I will answer his questions all at once. I want the world to know that this man who does not believe in God is trying to use a court in Tennessee — "

Darrow: "I object to that!"

Bryan: " — to slur at it, and while it will require time, I am willing to take it."

Darrow (shouting) : "I object to your statement. I am examining you on your fool ideas that no intelligent Christian on earth believes!"

Judge Raulston: "The court is adjourned!"

Next morning the judge ruled that the testimony in Darrow's cross-examination of Bryan was irrelevant, and ordered the trial to proceed. Darrow then arose and unexpectedly entered a plea of guilty for Scopes. The teacher was fined $100 and the trial was over.

By this quick maneuver on the part of the defense, Bryan was prevented from examining Darrow. However, Bryan had agreed with the judge that his own testimony given in answer to Darrow was irrelevant, so he consented to forego his turn at cross-examination. He did, however, earnestly ask the newspapermen to report the questions he would have asked Darrow, and most of them did so.

Later the case was appealed to the Tennessee Supreme Court with the intention of taking it on to the Supreme Court of the United States. But the state court upheld the constitutionality of the law, and to the surprise and disappointment of the defense attorneys nol-prossed the case, bringing to an end the epochal lawsuit.

Scopes, all his expenses paid by admirers, left the employ of the Rhea County High School and entered the University of Chicago. Later he went into business, working for an oil company in South America for a time, then moving to Louisiana.

Bryan was worn out by the emotional strain and the physical ardor of the trial. But his spirit was as vigorous as ever, keyed to a high point by the encounter through which he had passed. He felt that he had won a lasting moral victory, and the ridicule he had undergone apparently did not worry him. In his day he had been defeated three times for the presidency of the United States, by a small margin of votes, and had not been discouraged. Then he had fought for a national principle; now he had fought for his God.

From all parts of the local countryside came appeals by civic and religious groups for Bryan to speak. Four days after the trial ended, even though exhausted, he journeyed to Winchester, where he made a speech on the importance of Christianity. Next day he spoke at Cowan, the weather being so hot that his clothes were virtually drenched with perspiration. Then he returned to the home of Richard Rogers in Dayton, where he and his wife were staying. To Mrs. Bryan he spoke cheerfully of his work and of the results of the trial. On the next day, Sunday, July 26th, he lay down after the noonday meal to take a nap. He never awoke, passing away quietly in the little Tennessee town where he had come to wage his last great fight, in which he gave his life. Only five days before, in the midst of the trial, Bryan had said: "The Bible is all I need to live by and to die by."

The world was shocked and saddened by the sudden passing of the Great Commoner. The news dispatches about his death almost equaled the number sent out at the height of the trial. His body was taken to Washington and buried in Arlington National Cemetery, according to his own request. Thus in a doubly dramatic way the Dayton trial came to an end. It left a tremendous impression upon the country and the world. But its biggest and most lasting effects were on the people of the South, where it remains a milestone in their history. Some writers have implied that the trial was a shame and disgrace to the region. To those closest to the hearts of the Southern people, nothing could be more distant from reality.

When F. E. Robinson, owner of the drugstore where the trial had its origin, built himself another establishment some time after the trial was over, he observed that he had also acquired a new viewpoint as a result of the great event. To commemorate it, he carefully preserved in his new store, the table at which the trial was planned, plainly marked to show that here was born an event which resounded throughout the world. Looking back twenty-five years, Robinson observed:

> The trial got the local people better acquainted with the outside world. Because of this event, they got to know some of the nation's biggest men, especially prominent lawyers and writers. By reading what these writers wrote about the trial, the people here developed a habit of wider and more substantial reading in general — and therefore their

thinking was improved, something we pass on to our children. What impressed me most though, was what Mr. Bryan said, and its results. He predicted that it would be interesting to watch how much attention our people paid to the Bible after the trial had stimulated them into a new examination of science and literature. The results are: more people here are more deeply religious than ever before; and as far as their devotion to the Bible is concerned, they not only haven't gotten further away from it — many of them now carry it in public until the Good Book is as common an everyday sight as a shopping bag.

The trial itself was not commercialized. Bryan charged nothing for his services, bearing his own expenses. Darrow, whose fees usually ran into six figures, received a total of $83.27, a nickel of which, he explained, went to buy Bryan a ginger ale.

The attitude of the local people toward the visitors from the North and East who vilified them during the trial has come to be humorous and tolerant. It can perhaps be summed up in what a local county official, Squire B. M. Wilbur, said to a tourist who was passing through Dayton some time after the trial was over. He asked the squire directions, then looked around at the town and inquired:

"Are there many monkeys here?"

Without cracking a smile, the squire replied:

"No, but a lot of them pass through."

In his last speech, Bryan had said: "When a Christian wants to teach Christianity, he has to build his own college." These words were not in vain, although the Commoner never lived to see their consequences. Not long after the trial, a newspaperman who had covered it suggested that a university be built as an enduring memorial to William Jennings Bryan.

The proposal caught the fancy of many admirers, and soon plans were drawn. Upon a picturesque hill overlooking Dayton and its courthouse, Bryan University was founded, its educational policy based upon the fundamental beliefs of the Commoner. Eighty-two acres of beautiful Tennessee landscape was purchased, and work begun on the foundations of an impressive main building. From all parts of the world pledges of financial aid poured in, and for a time it looked as if a major university would spring up here. But the Depression changed this bright dream. Many who had given pledges found they could not fulfill them. Local people did what they could, but the stream of money soon dried up. It seemed as if the whole project would have to be abandoned. It was not, however. On September 18, 1930, in the midst of the Depression, Bryan University opened, not in cloistered halls but in the very room of the old courthouse where the Scopes Trial was held. For the next few years most of the classes of the new institution were held in the abandoned Rhea County High School building, and it may be noted that the first recitation of a class in Bible study took place in the same room where Scopes taught evolution. The university still uses his laboratory desk.

In 1935, Bryan University moved into its new main building on the hill, and since that time it has grown. By 1952 about three hundred students were enrolled.

The Legend of Maggie

On the sunny spring day of June 14, 1930, a goodly number of Cleveland clubwomen gathered to observe a colorful ceremony. The exact spot of the gathering was the old Harris

Mill, better known as "Maggie's Mill," located on Spring Creek, five miles south of Reliance in Polk County in the Unaka Range of the Smokies. These particular clubwomen were members of the Ocoee Chapter of the Daughters of the American Revolution, and their specific purpose was to unveil a marker to the storied heroine of the old song *When You and I Were Young, Maggie*. The day was beautiful, the ceremony impressive. The only trouble with the whole thing was that later, from another part of the continent, would come information to the effect that Maggie was never there.

But let us return respectfully to the scene of the unveiling. No such suspicions troubled the attendant throng. Wrote a reporter for the Cleveland *Banner:*

> The verdure-clad hills, the clear, rapidly-flowing stream, the dam and the old mill facing an assemblage of men, women and children held spellbound by the mystery of their surroundings, all contributed to a never-to-be-forgotten picture. Miss Jessie Rhea Gaut gave in her own inimitable manner the exquisite romance of Maggie Harris and her poet lover. . . . Following the telling of the incidents connected with the composition of George W. Johnson's poem, "When You and I Were Young Maggie," Mr. Robin Shugart played as a violin solo, J. A. Butterfield's setting of the poem which was later sung with touching effect by Mr. Ralph Swartz. . . . Mrs. D. B. Todd of Etowah stood framed in the doorway a few feet above the singers, a perfect replica of an ante-bellum beauty, correctly attired as she was in a many-flounced, rose-colored, silk, hoop-skirted gown, a flower-decorated poke bonnet, black lace mitts and frilled pantalettes.
>
> Mr. Thomas Taylor of Etowah, owner of the mill, accepted in well-chosen words the marker tendered by the Ocoee chapter. . . . At the conclusion of his remarks, Mr. Taylor unveiled the marker which consists of one of the

millstones set in native stone above a slab of pink sandstone
on which the following is cut:

> "The song 'When You and I Were Young Maggie'
> was written here and dedicated to his wife,
> Maggie Harris, by her husband, George Johnson
> in 1820."

Alas, these fine sentiments were to wither from humorous
ridicule, and the purple prose to pale into words of a travesty.
Not, however, for several years, and not until thousands of
tourists had been duly escorted up the small, winding roads
beyond the town of Cleveland to view the impressive D.A.R.
marker these ladies had erected in genuine tribute to the
tears of a saddened lover. Some local audiences even stood in
reverence when the song was played or sung. The late P. B.
Mayfield, eminent Cleveland attorney and benefactor, once
told this writer that he grew so tired of friends and relatives
asking him to be taken to Maggie's Mill that he got so he
would just take them up the road a way until he came to the
first mill he saw, and then say solemnly: "There it is." Apparently they never knew the difference.

Literature was printed about the old mill, and postcards
showing it were sold to tourists with considerable success.
The governor of Tennessee, Henry H. Horton, even got on
the Maggie bandwagon and duly dedicated the structure in
the name of the great Volunteer State. From all parts of the
country, people who had heard of Maggie's Mill came to see,
and carried back home stories about the picturesque setting
for the composition of the song. One of these accounts reached
the ears of Donald H. Johnson of Seattle. He wrote to the
president-general of the D.A.R. in Washington, D.C., stating
that he was a relative of the composer of the song and denouncing the Tennessee claim to Maggie's Mill as a hoax.

The people who lived round the site were asked to prove that it was authentic (they never did). Johnson then went on to inform the spellbound D.A.R. that he was the grand-nephew of George W. Johnson, author of the words of the song, and that to his certain knowledge the latter was never in Tennessee. According to him, George W. Johnson was born in Ontario, Canada, at a little town named Hall's Corners, near which, at the foot of Dudass Mountain, was located an old mill, the real scene of the creation of the song. The author married Maggie Clark, a resident of the same Canadian neighborhood, who died less than a year later, therefore the sad theme.

The poem which the bereaved Johnson had written about his beloved wife came to the attention of J. A. Butterfield, who wrote the melody for it and made a fortune from its success; Johnson never received any money at all. According to the music historian Sigmund Spaeth, Butterfield was an Englishman who came to this country and became a conductor and composer. Of the approximately one hundred fifty songs which he wrote, only *Maggie* was a popular success, selling over 250,000 copies from 1866, the year of its composition and publication, to 1885.

The Ocoee Chapter reeled; but there was more proof to come. Mrs. Elizabeth D. Badgham of Bloomfield, New Jersey, announcing that she was the youngest sister of the Maggie Clark referred to by Donald H. Johnson, also charged that the Tennessee story of the mill was false. She said that the mill was on her father's farm in Canada, and that the husband of her sister Maggie, George W. Johnson, onetime editor of the Cleveland (Ohio) *Plain-Dealer,* wrote the song for his wife, who died after a year of happy marriage.

Finally, in 1934, Colonel C. R. McCullough, historian and

founder of the Canadian Club, confirmed that Maggie was actually the late Maggie Clark of the Township of Glanford in Wentworth County, Ontario. This claim was substantiated by the naturalist Robert Sparks Walker of Chattanooga, and by the Musical Division of the Library of Congress.

Henry Ford, who made a hobby of buying old landmarks and moving them to his Michigan estate, had become interested in Maggie's Mill, but the revelations from Canada changed the auto magnate's mind. How the Tennessee claim to Maggie originated is hard to determine. John S. Chamblin of Cleveland (Tenn.) related that a Bob Johnson owned some land adjoining the old mill, which itself was the property of a John Harris. The then-general belief that it really *was* Maggie's Mill enhanced the value of the real estate, so no denial was made by the owners — according to this version. They probably boosted it. At any rate, when Maggie's devoted mate "wandered . . . to the hills," they evidently were Canadian and not part of the Smokies.

The Melungeons

There was a time in the Smoky Mountain Country when mothers scared their children by saying: "The Melungeons will get you if you don't watch out." The frightened youngsters, envisioning some sort of big ghoulish goblins afoot in the land, would hide under the bedcovers a-shiver with fright.

There were Melungeons, all right, but they were real people and not particularly scary. The first records of them date back to 1784, when the State of Franklin was formed from North Carolina territory, and a colony of strange people with dark complexions of a reddish-brown hue was found in the upper Smokies. They were said by some to be descended from the Moors; by others, to be a mixed breed of Indians and Negroes; while still others looked upon them as being a mixture of red, black, and white. They called themselves Melungeons.

The great-great-grandchildren of these people still live in East Tennessee and Virginia, mainly to themselves; and no one has yet ascertained their true origin. The present-day Melungeons claim to be of Portuguese descent — pronouncing the word "Porter-gee." The name "Melungeon" is said by some scholars to derive from the French *mélange*, meaning mixture. In any case, fascinating legends persist about these unusual people, because there is just enough lack of positive evidence about their origin and race to give credence to the unusual. Years ago the story circulated that the Melungeons were descended from the lost colony of Roanoke, founded by Sir Walter Raleigh in Virginia only to vanish completely. Another legend was to the effect that they were the offspring of a group of Spanish voyagers who were shipwrecked off the North Carolina coast and wandered inland.

The men are tall and straight, with high cheekbones and small, sharp eyes usually black or gray. The generally known fact that Indians always have black eyes would indicate that the Melungeons are not of their origin. The women are small, less than the average in height, with dark eyes and coal-black hair. They too have high cheekbones. Both men and women have a swarthy complexion. The hands of the women are dainty and shapely, as are their little feet in spite of much walking over the mountain trails; and since the Negro slaves had large feet and hands, it is unlikely the Melungeons were part of some African tribe, as has been suggested. They are

Christian in their religion, and extreme pacifists; the early ones would fight neither for the Indians nor for the white settlers.

Until 1834 the Melungeons enjoyed all the rights of citizenship, but the Tennessee state convention of that year disfranchised all persons of color, including these unfortunate mulatto-like people. After this loss of privilege, the Melungeons took to the hills and became literally a lost colony. They were soon a law unto themselves. In resentment against the white people who had ostracized them, they became a terror to the other settlers of the hills. They would slip out of their mountain fastness and steal cattle, food, and furniture. Not content with minor pillaging, they learned to counterfeit money, and became adept at this illegal practice — though how they learned the technique and where they got their equipment and metal no one seems to know. It is possible that they found gold and silver in the mountain streams, for both have since been discovered there. In point of fact, their counterfeit coins, which easily passed for real money, actually contained more gold and silver than those of the federal government. Near the Kentucky line in East Tennessee today may be seen ruins of ancient furnaces believed to have been used for smelting by the early Melungeons. (Another illicit pursuit at which men of this mysterious tribe excelled was the distilling of brandy. At one time or another, it is said, virtually every Melungeon male engaged in this practice.)

Writing in the *Arkansas Gazette* of January 14, 1912, Mrs. Eliza N. Heiskell treated the Melungeons in a charitable vein:

> As a class, they are faithful friends. They have a kindly nature and their personal friendship carries a degree of unselfishness that could well be imitated in higher life. They

never presumed to be on an equal with the whites but were content to occupy an intermediate ground between them and the Negro slaves. They are a shrinking, timid people outside their own boundaries. During the Civil War a few of them were in the Southern armies but most of them were loyal to the Union. . . . In one respect, the Melungeons are like the Irish peasants in that one of their principal recreations consists in telling and hearing stories, recounting famous neighborhood fights and tales of hunting adventures. They also have many superstitions. They have a firm belief in the powerful influence of the moon and a never-failing fear of "haints."

The records of Hancock County in 1813, however, tell a different story. A number of the Melungeons lived in that locality, and had become conspicuous by their dirtiness and illiteracy. Whenever they chanced to appear in public, they squatted instead of standing or sitting. If invited into anyone's house, they would spit great pools of tobacco juice on the floor. They were regarded as extremely immoral, according to the county clerk's record, yet were said to be "great shouters and advocates of religion." They were so curious about the doings of white people that they would stalk a visitor to their haunts for miles through the woods, trying to find out the object of the visit. In the burial rites of their dead they exercised unusual reverence, following the body for miles to the grave, on foot and in single file.

Although their citizenship was restored in 1859, the Melungeons still remain an anomalous race. They are set apart as much by their queer and untidy customs and shrinking attitude, their illiteracy and isolation, as by the color of their skin.

The late Judge Lewis Lewis Shepherd, a well-known Chattanooga attorney, once defended a Melungeon girl in a famous trial. She was accused by relatives of being part Negro, and therefore, because of the allegedly illegal marriage of her parents, not entitled to inherit their property. Judge Shepherd won the case, and his description of the Melungeons has come down as colorful, interesting, and perhaps to some extent authentic. He contended that they were descendants of the ancient Phoenicians who built the city of Carthage and whose leader was Hannibal. After the fall of this city to the Romans, the Phoenicians settled in Morocco, from where they crossed over to Gibraltar and eventually arrived in Portugal. Shakespeare's Othello supposedly came from this group of people. Then, according to the Shepherd account, a part of the colony crossed the Atlantic and settled in the northern part of South Carolina, whence they moved over into the country which is now East Tennessee.

In Lee County, Virginia, which adjoins Hancock County, Tennessee, about five hundred Melungeons live today, mostly as farm laborers. Some of these have acquired farms, and show signs of improving their status. Another group lives in Graysville, Tennessee, a village of Rhea County, where they constitute about thirty-five per cent of the population. This entire colony is known by the surname of Goins.* Most of them live in shacks on the edge of the village, and work in mines or on farms.

The Melungeons like bright colors; their children, even the boys, attend Sunday school with red ribbons in their hair. Reverend William Leonard, pastor of the Vardy Springs Church in Hancock County, said that although Melungeons attend his services regularly, "they like to backslide about

---

* The Melungeons ordinarily follow a peculiar method of naming. For example, the wife of one named George Henry is known as Elizabeth George. Their son is called Jack George, their daughter, Emily George, and so on, using the father's first name where we employ the surname.

every two years and join another church." He has usually ignored such defections and accepted them again as members of his congregation, when they wanted to return. Most of the Melungeons in this county of upper East Tennessee live in squalid homes, though some in recent years have shown a tendency to improve their mode of existence. Less than twenty years ago, one family was found living in a one-room log cabin without a single window, the only openings being the chimney and the solitary door. Two iron beds, one home-made cot, a rough table, an ancient step-stove, and two chairs wired together to keep either from falling, constituted the furniture of the household. The head of the family, a known drunkard, had gotten intoxicated the week before the visit of a Civil Works Administration researcher to the cabin, gone to sleep by the fireplace, caught fire and had his clothes burned off him, causing serious injury. His wife, going fran-tically across the mountains in search of medical aid, died from a heart attack en route. The seven children, all under sixteen, were found by the public authorities to be in need of food, and did not have sufficient clothing to attend the funeral of their mother, this being hastily provided by the CWA in time for the sad service.

The Melungeons are said to be sexually precocious, and certainly large numbers of them marry at a very early age and have countless children. Among the group in Hancock County, illegitimacy is high. But apparently the women are capable of the hard life and constant childbearing. In a letter from Mrs. Rebecca Daugherty to the historian John Trot-wood Moore, dated January 23, 1923, is found the following comment about Melungeon women: "Their endurance is al-most unbelievable. It is nothing for one of the grandmothers to remark that she believes she 'will walk over to Zeke's tomorrer,' a matter of 40-odd miles over two mountains."

One of the most famous — or notorious — Melungeons was Mahala Mullins, who lived with her numerous children in a log cabin on Newman's Ridge in Hancock County for many years, carrying on her favorite activity of bootlegging. She was not arrested, and the reason was simple: she was so fat, weighing around seven hundred pounds, that the revenue officers could not get her through the cabin door. Her story is told succinctly but clearly by an old mountaineer neighbor:

"She sot there on that bed for years and sold liquor out of the barrel settin' beside her. The law would go up there to arrest her. She would say to them, 'Here I am. Take me if ye can.' She was so fat that them men couldn't budge her. And when she died, they had to knock the fireplace out of the end of her cabin to git her out to bury her."

IX

Boom But Mainly Bust

Fortune smiled on the Smoky Mountain Country as the 1920's wore on. Prosperity blessed the farmer and small businessman, many of whom had supported the stoical Vermont Republican in the White House and were surprised when he did not "choose to run" again. Prices for their products had risen after the war and had not gone down, and the advent of the inexpensive automobile, the tractor, and a few good roads made life more pleasant indeed.*

Not many people of this section owned stocks of the New York Exchange but when the great bubble burst in 1929 they certainly felt the effects. At first it seemed like some faraway catastrophe, then slowly its economic effects filtered

---

* The roads through this section of the country were often in bad shape. Even the so-called highways through the valleys were rough and rutted, and in some seasons of the year so muddy that the early motorists had a hard time getting through, often having to be pulled out of the mudholes with mules or horses. There is the story of one Yankee tourist who had bogged down in the sticky clay of a Monroe County road and had paid ten dollars to be pulled out by a local farmer with his team of mules. Just before he drove off, the motorist remarked:

"I should think you'd be pulling people out of this stuff day and night."

"Nope," drawled the farmer, "at night's when we tote the water to wet the roads."

down through the operations of the big corporations which had Southern branches. The slowdown in buying of consumer products caused local plants to close, and many of the rural people who had moved into town were thrown out of work. In Washington the national government made valiant efforts to stem the ebbing economic tide, some of which were to be credited to the next administration; but the swing had been too wide. The lowering economic curve gathered momentum on its downward rush, and before it reached bottom had ushered in the greatest depression the country has ever known. It caused many local families to leave their poor-paying farms and go to the city in search of relief; conversely, many left the cities to hunt up country cousins whose larders were not yet empty and who still had a sort of roof over their heads.

The general standard of living was directly affected by the lowering of purchasing power in all commodities. The farmers could not buy, therefore the business firms suffered, and many closed their doors. The stepped-up installment buying of the 'twenties had loaded many a small family with high-priced furniture, especially grand pianos, the remains of many of which can still be seen in and near their homes. Radios and refrigerators were other items, while in the garage sat a new car also purchased on the "a little down, a little each month" plan. Now with less money coming in, payments were allowed to lapse. In some cases this resulted in the items being reclaimed by the sellers; in others, the merchants tried to get along without such drastic measures. But in either case bankruptcy was common, especially among the smaller firms with little capital for cushioning the shock. Freight rates fell less rapidly than prices, which worked still another hardship on the shippers. The volume of agricultural exports declined sharply and abnormal surpluses resulted, notably in flue-cured tobacco.*

By 1932 business activity had fallen to forty per cent below normal, worse than at any time since the Panic of 1893. This low level held until 1936, when New Deal pump-priming measures began to raise it. In seven Tennessee counties, including some in East Tennessee, credit corporations which had held only eight farms in 1922 held two hundred ninety-seven by 1936. Part of this insolvency was caused by the too-liberal lending policies of some "big-hearted but impractical banks" before the national bank holiday of 1933, and part was caused by the downtrend in the general price level and the increase in cash farm expenditures. Mechanization on the farms was held back by the lack of available capital at low rates of interest.

A survey of Hawkins County in East Tennessee showed a typical food deficiency. Sixty-three per cent of the families there ate pork every day, and no beef whatever. In other counties there was not enough milk for the children, or enough butter and eggs for anyone. Houses were in dire need of roof-repair, better lighting, and painting. Bare yards and outdoor privies added to the unfavorable conditions. Lack of pasture crops limited the supply of dairy cows, and the decreasing number of home gardens, caused by the cost of seeds, was another problem in the average economy.

Insurance policies were dropped by the thousands. Home life was disrupted by the departure of unhappy members of the families for such reasons as: to reduce rents; bankruptcy; a job in town; inability of owners of land to pay wages;

---

* Symbolic of the Depression days was a cheap smoking tobacco used in the region and known as "Hoover Dust." Its quality was not the highest but it was the best a lot of the boys could afford, and they rolled their cigarettes from it whereas formerly they had reveled in "ready rolls."

owner wanted cash for rent; house was burned; tenant was laid off by the landlord; mortgage was foreclosed on the farm; too many city relatives had crowded into the farmhouse. In one East Tennessee county, two out of three families were found to have moved one or more times between 1930 and 1935, according to a study made by Dr. W. E. Cole, professor of sociology at the University of Tennessee. This study also revealed that many homes lost their furniture during the Depression; that in a great number of cases, three or more persons slept together in one bed; that there was a lack of fuel in winter; that clothing was generally inadequate, underwear ragged or entirely lacking, shoes worn out, and many children therefore having to stay out of school; and that much illness resulted from the general lack of the necessities of life.

At this time conditions in the area which was to form the great Norris Dam basin of the Tennessee Valley Authority were a mixture of the progressive and backward, with emphasis upon the latter. There was one telephone for every thirty families. On an average, men married between the ages of twenty-one and twenty-three, women between eighteen and nineteen. Divorces were rare. The average size of families was 4.4, ten per cent higher than the national average for rural areas. Half of the families had sewing machines. Water for drinking was carried on an average of 58.9 yards. Seventy-one per cent of the families used washtubs for bathing; some used only creeks or rivers. One-third of the families had no toilet facilities. Two-thirds of the families owned and operated farms, but the average annual net cash income was $100 per person, and ten per cent of the 19,736 families were on relief. Soon the vision of a few statesmen was to bring a great advancement to this region, but in the early 'thirties it had reached a new low.

The Coming of TVA

More than a depression had struck the region in and around the Smoky Mountains. There was a change of life. The old order, held onto so closely and fondly by the settlers for so many years, was at last slipping away. A system that even a world war could not destroy was being eaten up by an economic recession.

Most of the farmers had not progressed far from the axe and single-tongue plow stage. Fertilizer was expensive, and electric power unavailable to the poorer people in the off-road sections. Even the farmers in the valleys were getting along on an average income of $100 a year, and the mountain men thought ten bushels of corn to the acre was a right good crop. It was not that they were ignorant. They just couldn't help themselves. Corn, cotton, and tobacco, the "summer row crops," were about the only ones they could grow on their land. The fertilizer they ordinarily used was not the right kind, but a temporary expedient to help make the crop. County agents had told them so, and they agreed, but they did not have the money to buy the improved fertilizers recommended or even to carry their farms over the periods necessary for conversion to better productivity. Not being able to start improvement, they became discouraged and disinterested in it, and kept on growing the same things year after year, causing erosion and exhaustion of their soil. As the Depression years passed, the land became more and more deficient in minerals. The woodlands were depleted by excessive cutting and frequent burning, and few attempts at reforestation had been made. Devastating floods played havoc along the course of the Tennessee River and its tributaries.

Then into this somber situation, in 1933, came something which was to change the entire social picture of the hill country and its adjoining territory: the Tennessee Valley Authority, born of the vision of Nebraska's Senator George W. Norris, who had fought for a decade to bring fruitful order out of the chaotic aftermath of Muscle Shoals, and implemented by President Franklin D. Roosevelt, who believed the TVA would be considered his most lasting contribution to the people of the South, even of the United States.

In brief, the new enterprise was to effect tremendous strides in navigation, flood control, electric power, malaria control, recreation, stream sanitation, fishing, forestry, and agriculture. TVA was to revive some of the deteriorated economy and literally light the way to a new life. But when the federal government first moved in there was an upheaval felt from Newfound Gap to the Cumberland Plateau. The first step in its operations was to build a dam on the Clinch River at its gorge near the town of Clinton. This structure, located in a picturesque natural setting, rose within a few months to a height of 265 feet and a length of 1860 feet, and the local folks had never seen the like of it. Soon the great Norris Dam looked down upon the people with the domination of a sphinx, disturbing and disrupting in its significance and activity.

Behind the dam, water was to back up over 37,000 acres of Tennessee land; and this was when the tumult began. The social conditions among the people living in the Norris basin have already been described; yet their attitude can be summed up in one sentence: none wanted to leave. The TVA set up a system of appraising and purchasing the land that was eminently fair, but at the time no method of separation would have been viewed as equitable by the thousands affected. After field appraisers made their report on a farm, it was submitted to a nonpartisan committee of experts familiar with the local land, which then recommended the price the government should offer. The owner could take this or leave it. If he rejected it, the government brought condemnation proceedings, but only as a last resort. Actually no more than five per cent of the families involved took the matter into court. Most of them, when they saw the new "water marks" on their trees, gave in gracefully if tearfully, and left. The TVA was careful, however, to relocate people as near to their old homes as possible.

The removal was not so bad for the young people. Their ties in the Norris basin as well as in other TVA areas were not particularly strong, and many of them regarded the move as an adventure with interesting possibilities. But with the older folks it was different. They had spent their lives on their family land and, poor or not, it was home to them, a much-loved domicile that could never be replaced. Some of them have never become reconciled. Don Whitehead of the Associated Press wrote, after visiting among them in 1941:

> Most of the families have moved to better farms. Their economic situation is sounder, and social conditions have improved with the coming of electricity and modern conveniences. And yet there is no real contentment because of the nagging memories. . . . They had their roots deep in the soil of their old homesteads. But they can never return.

A local farmer put it a little differently. "Did you ever see a hog turned out from a muddy pen to high dry ground?" he asked. "He'll go back to the muddy pen every time, if he can. We're something like that."

In Pleasant View Cemetery near Maynardville, Tennessee, there is a tombstone inscription that is revealing:

Major Allen Hurst
son of
John and Elizabeth Thompson Hurst
March 4, 1810, Tazewell Co. Virginia
May 26, 1873
First Circuit Court Clerk of Union County

During Reconstruction Days Robbed by
the Carpet Baggers of 4,000 acres.
60-odd years later the TVA
Confiscated Several Thousand acres
of Mineral Land left
to his Grandchildren
GONE WITH THE WIND

But TVA was not heartless; an example of its consideration occurred at Dandridge. There elderly Mrs. Anna Hynds had a spring of water which flowed through the yard of her home. For centuries, she told the TVA men, this spring had been in her family, secure in its cool, little cove from which issued crystal-clear water. Now the efficient thing for the TVA to have done would have been to plug up the spring so as not to interfere with the nearby lake, which was filling from a dam. Instead, out of consideration for the feelings of Mrs. Hynds, the men installed a pump to lift the spring water over the wall and into the lake.

Classic is the case of the man who lived in a log cabin where a fire burned perpetually in the fireplace. He said the fire had been in his family for three generations and had never been allowed to go out — and he did not intend for it to go out now. TVA solved the problem by moving the man and his blazing fire intact.

Slightly different is the story of a bootlegger who was living contentedly in the Smoky Mountains, operating his still beside a roaring creek, when the National Park Service bought up all the land around for the new national park. The 'legger had to move. He went to Union County, where he resumed his occupation of making moonshine. After being here a few years, the TVA moved in and took his land for the Norris Dam basin. He next moved down on the Clinch River, and there was again engaged in his favorite vocation when the Oak Ridge project came along. This was the last straw.

"Used to be, the only federal men I dealt with was the revenooers," he snorted, "and we understood each other. Now it seems that every time I come home from a run, they's a guvermint man a-settin' on my doorstep with papers orderin' me to move. Ef I knowed of a place where there weren't no guvermint men but revenooers, I'd shore go there."

The problems which TVA had to solve were numberless and numbing. One of the most difficult was the moving of graves, of which there were five thousand in the Norris basin alone, many of them in small family graveyards located, from affection, near the houses. The thought of having their loved ones submerged under two hundred feet of water impelled the people to insist that the graves be properly removed. The government men had to study hundreds of death records, in order to track down and consult widely scattered relatives about the disposition of remains. Reverently the bones were dug up, occasionally with a family group attending as if gathering for a second funeral. New caskets were provided, as was transportation to non-inundatable cemetery sites. At the new location a preacher, also provided by TVA if desired, held a brief reinterment ceremony. Either the old gravestone was set up again, or a new one was furnished. One owner of a family cemetery made the unusual request that his little graveyard be left where it was and buoys placed in the water to indicate the site. The TVA declined.

Displaced persons were not the only ones to kick about TVA. Disconnected stockholders did too. In the region was a flourishing public utilities concern, the Tennessee Electric Power Company. It was a subsidiary of the big Commonwealth & Southern Corporation in New York, headed by Wendell Willkie, who fought TVA tooth and nail with all his vigorous prowess. There were also local stockholders who did not wish to see their prosperous company taken over by the government, and local employees who did not desire to see their jobs go by the Power Board, as the TVA supervising agency was to be called. They brought suit against TVA, tried to stop it, and, failing that, endeavored to delay. There were bitter feelings in the region, erstwhile best friends taking different sides, and newspapers entering the public-power fight pro and con. One, the time-honored Chattanooga *News*, headed by George Fort Milton, conducted a losing battle against the Tennessee Electric Power Company, lost much of its advertising, and eventually, with other factors contributing, went under, in spite of all its loyal personnel could do. In the final stages of the fight, Willkie sold the utilities company to the government for $78,000,000.

The early struggles of TVA were as nothing, however, compared to the changes it wrought. First of all, it brought electric power where it had never been available before. Probably next in importance was the cheap fertilizer it provided farmers. At a conference on soil erosion held soon after the advent of TVA, two preachers happened to be present. One, in thankfulness, began to talk about "soul erosion," and declared: "I'm going back home and preach phosphate and limestone instead of hellfire and brimstone." The other minister remarked solemnly: "The greatest thing that can happen to a man, in my opinion, is to have Jesus Christ in his heart. But the next greatest thing is electricity."

And as far as the Smoky Mountain Country was concerned, he spoke the truth. Before TVA there was electricity on only one farm out of every twenty-five; ten years later, one out of every five had it; and at this writing it seems that just about every cabin in the hills has the light and power that make life more livable. What were the conditions of only two decades ago? Coal-oil lamps in the house, lanterns carried to the barn at night and early morning, refrigeration by cooling milk and butter in the spring house, drinking and washing water carried considerable distances, and the smelly, inconvenient, insanitary outdoor privies are but a few of the things which quickly come to mind. James Whitcomb Riley may have cherished the memory of the old wooden toilets at the edge of the yard enough to write a poem about them, but if he were living today he would certainly have modern plumbing and thank his muse for it. A recent visit which I made to a country relative points up the difference. There are now a refrigerator and stove in the kitchen, both electric, the former saving many backbreaking steps as well as being vastly more efficient, the latter replacing the big, clumsy, oldfashioned wood-burning range which heated the cook and kitchen almost as much as it did the food, and made summer cooking an ordeal. Instead of weary, aching human hands, an electric pump now carries water up the long hill from the spring. On the back porch an electric washing machine takes the place of black iron kettles in the yard and exhausting hand rubbing on the washboard. An electric ironer makes a memory of countless hours of bending over the old board wielding a crude flatiron heated at intervals on the wood stove. Also on the back porch is a big deep-freezing locker full of chicken, ham, steak, bacon, and other homegrown meats, as well as every variety of green vegetable fresh from the nearby garden, perfectly preserved by electric refrigeration for use months after the time they were placed inside. No more need for the endless home canning which Mother sweated through on torrid summer days when she should have been resting. The spanking white bathroom with its modern porcelain fixtures, made possible by an up-to-date water supply, has relegated to comic books the surreptitious scurry to the distant outhouse, there to sit with the remaining pages of the Sears, Roebuck catalog, chilled in winter and scorched in summer. Among the other appliances these country kinfolks glory in are food dehydrators, motors to grind feed at the barn, electricity to cut wood, turn lathes, cure hams, process sweet potatoes, and cool and pasteurize milk, besides providing bright and plentiful light at night for all the farm and home activities. Truly the hard, dark days of pioneer living which stayed with this region well through the Depression years have gone.

Before TVA, the land was tired. The monotonous row crops had taken their dismal toll, and good soil from many a hillside lay useless in the Gulf of Mexico, carried sixteen hundred miles by the Tennessee, Ohio, and Mississippi rivers. With TVA, dams high in the mountains helped control the flow of water, retarding the erosion that had gone on since the time when trees grew on the slopes and held the rich soil in place. Government officials showed the farmers how to change their crops, take the corn, cotton, and tobacco from the hillsides and plant it on the level lands below, where dirt and dust collect and stay and the thieves of erosion do not break through and steal. The farmers were shown that grass planted on the slopes was not only good for holding the soil but excellent pasture as well. Across the gullies that were already too deep to erase quickly, check-dams were built by CCC boys. Brush was used to dam the large gullies, the small ones were plowed up. The future of the lumber industry in the area was at stake, and millions of saplings were planted in denuded forest areas, which before long began to develop into rich and protecting small woodlands.

County agents had talked about building up worn soil. Now TVA actually furnished the fertilizer. Sacks of life-giving phosphates to augment the lime rock were dumped onto hungry land and gratefully utilized; thousands of farm families were found willing to risk a change in their venerated farming methods and undertake a new way of agricultural life. In cooperation with TVA, the state universities, and the always-helpful county agents, they let their acres become demonstration farms which tested new fertilizers and farm and home improvements. By 1942, egg, milk, livestock, and pasture production had increased from twenty-one to thirty per cent. In the Birds Community of Sevier County, Tennessee, for example, the yield of corn was increased fifty-seven per cent by the new fertilizer, and the number of milk cows increased from forty-three to seventy-three head within six years because of the doubled grazing capacity of pastures on which lime and phosphate had been used.

A traveler from the North once passed through East Tennessee and remarked, with that aplomb typical of the Johnny-come-lately who leaves early, that he knew what was the matter with Southern people: they all had malaria. But this remark did have a basis in fact. In some sections two-thirds of the people were affected by this sickness; and the overall average, when TVA came in, was about one-fourth of the population. It presented a problem to be reckoned with, especially since the new dams threatened to produce more malarial mosquitoes, the many miles of shallow water around the edges of their lakes making perfect breeding places. One method used to combat this situation was to drop the level of the lakes by mechanical means, thus leaving the larvae stranded and dying on the dry land. But this was expensive and impractical, and also interfered with power production of the dams, so other means were eventually devised, such as spraying DDT on the water from airplanes, controlling the vegetation along the banks, and making the edges of the lakes sheer and uninviting to the mosquitoes. When the TVA experts were working to eliminate *Anopheles quadrimaculatus,* which they nicknamed "Annies," they caught and sprayed some with a pink solution in order to discover where and how far they flew, and how often they moved from one spot to another. Local folks chancing to find some of these "pink Annies" were at first flabbergasted, then, when they found out the reason for the color, commented with amusement and chagrin on the government's "wastin' the people's money on catchin' and paintin' dad-burned muskeeters." New insecticides stronger than DDT are being developed and used, and, all in all, the TVA work toward eliminating malaria has had wonderful results. In 1950, the agency made blood tests of forty-three hundred individuals in the areas where the disease once flourished, and every one was negative. Thus in one generation has malaria ceased to be a determining factor.

Along the rivers and lakes of the TVA territory are over ten thousand miles of shoreline offering opportunities for recreation. In 1934 there was no state park system in Tennessee or no state department of conservation, and not a single county had made provision for park areas. This has all been changed. With the help of the TVA, Tennessee has established an excellent department of conservation, much of whose work is in the Smoky Mountain region, where the natural advantages of scenery and wildlife, all within five hundred miles or two days' driving time of more than half the population of the nation, has made it a great tourist mecca.

In the beginning TVA constructed several demonstration parks, such as Big Ridge Park near the now-inundated village of Loyston just west of Knoxville. The many persons who soon visited this and other new parks liked them, and their advantages, advertised in attractive brochures by TVA, spread across the country. There are bathing beaches, campsites, vacation cottages, stores, restaurants, and boat docks for the numerous pleasure craft which ply up and down the great new waterways of the refashioned region. In addition to the government-built facilities, there have sprung up countless privately owned tourist camps, roadside souvenir stands, and streamlined honky-tonks. Altogether over four million dollars had been spent by mid-century on tourist accommodations in the region.

The fish and game at first had a holiday. Their number was replenished by government restocking, and strict rules were clamped on fishing and hunting. It was not long, however, before the streams and lakes were so full of fish, and the woods so full of animals, that these restrictions could be relaxed. All seasons were opened for fishing. For the angler and nimrod, the Smoky Mountain Country is now paradise.

Not without reason did John Gunther write that TVA was "the biggest contribution the United States has yet made to society in the modern world." There was good cause for a Southern newspaper reporter to state that "the significant advance has been made in the thinking of the people. They are no longer afraid. They have caught the vision of their own powers." In the opinion of most, TVA has already fulfilled a great mission. But a vociferous minority has continued to assail it. Some of the displaced farmers have contended that it was not necessary to inundate so much of their land; that now their best bottomland is gone, buried under six hundred thousand acres of water. Others have stated that with AAA, state, and county assistance, and the cooperation of the U.S. Department of Agriculture, farm prosperity has come anyway — would have come to the Smoky Mountain Country without TVA. Other government agencies have felt that TVA got credit for progress in navigation, flood control, erosion control, reforestation, and distribution of electric power which was partly due to their own efforts. Shouts of "paternalistic government subsidy" have been hurled at the TVA "yardstick" for providing cheaper power, pointing out that TVA pays no extremely high salaries and bonuses and does not have to satisfy investors. Criticism reached a climax in the charges of Frank Chodorov that "we now have the truth about TVA: it is not an economic instrument for the betterment of the country . . . it is only an idea. What is that idea? Just Socialism."

Most folks in the Smokies do not entertain ideas interwoven with higher economics or political systems. What they do know is that they have better roads, more lights, a lot of new electrical gadgets which made life easier and happier; and that their land and rivers are being put to better use than ever. One of their "boys" in Washington, Estes Kefauver, even suggested more TVA's, right after the big floods in Missouri in 1951 that did billions of dollars' worth of damage. He pointed out that such things don't happen in the Tennessee Valley any more. Democrats and Republicans differ in this section, as they do everywhere else. But on one thing they are pretty well in agreement: TVA is OK.

The CCC

A dynamic factor in reshaping Tennessee-Carolina, one that has never received proper credit, was the Civilian Conservation Corps. In 1933, after the CCC was set up, there rolled into this upland section hordes of young men from other parts of the country, especially from the lower East Side of New York. Mixed with them in the camps that spotted the TVA area was a sprinkling of local fellows, some of them from far back in the mountains. It was a novel experience for the Northern boys, to say the least; they had read of hillbillies and their mountain homes, but it was something else to live with and among them. Their mission in the region was to clear the way for TVA dams, build recreation parks, stop soil erosion, and do reforestation. There was nothing in their agreement with Uncle Sam which said they had to get along with the "yokels of the hills." But the New York Irish, Italians, and Jews soon learned to respect the local men, whom they found completely at home in this great, healthful outdoors where an active new life was opening up with pick and shovel, axe and jack-hammer, truck and bulldozer.* Too, the Southern boys had sisters, some of whom the newcomers respected, others of whom fell into a category the nature of which may be inferred from the words of an anxious father to a CCC camp commander:

"I want that feller O'Flynn to come back over to my house, prepared to take supper and several other meals. He's a-marryin' my daughter or I'll use this here hog rifle on him — that's fer shore!"

After a number of such incidents, the local people came to resent the "furrin three C boys," and many would not allow them in their homes. Gradually, however, after the worst members of the corps were weeded out or voluntarily went over the hill, the rest gained a new respect in the minds of the natives. They themselves developed more regard for the people who lived on this land, and as a result there were many orthodox marriages, the new sons-in-law usually remaining to live on the farms after their tour of CCC duty expired.

Almost two decades after the CCC began its work in these hills, the results can be seen reaching full fruition. That neat, picturesque roadside or lakeside park with its cozy, pioneer-type cabins, its stone masonry, its well-kept trees and winding trails, may bear the name of some other government agency, but it was probably built by the CCC boys back in the days when joining the corps was more honorable than being on relief or living off the old man. Many of the roads

* A burly mess sergeant from New York who was known as a bully one day insulted a tall, slender young mountaineer in one of the Norris Basin CCC camps. The latter invited him outside. Grabbing his kitchen butcher knife, the sergeant roared through the doorway, swearing that he would "cut the daylights out of that lousy hick." But his boast proved a bit erroneous. The slender boy let him take one great swing at him with the knife, deftly stepped aside, then with his fists redesigned the mess sergeant's face, breaking his nose and closing his eyes. The sergeant was hospitalized, the mountaineer discharged, but the incident improved relations all around.

and steep trails in the national parks were hewn out of wilderness by these Depression-struck young men who pushed bulldozers into the brush, then followed up with mattocks and sledgehammers as they clung to the rocky sides of the mountains. Across once-eroded fields and hillsides, covered with grass and molded gracefully into the landscape, are thousands of terraces which once were only dirt on the shovels of CCC boys. In the half-denuded forests where predatory lumber interests once operated, paying no attention to the future of the woods, the corps planted millions of seedlings that are today young forests in themselves. Some people joked about the CCC, called it "uniform relief," and felt it to be a waste of New Deal money. But the long-term effects of its work, in this section at least, indicate that the money was well invested, and that the relief was of a permanent type.

A Settlement School

In 1912 the national college sorority Pi Beta Phi founded a settlement school for local children in Gatlinburg. The purpose of the school, which has since become a thriving institution, was set forth as follows: ". . . to develop initiative and independence among the mountain people and to foster home industries which might become a means of livelihood." A principal difference between this school and some of the well-meaning but often condescending "missions" that have been attempted by other organizations, is that the sorority officials took a realistic approach and did not talk down to the local people.

The first member of the sorority to go among the natives was referred to initially as "that woman." They wanted to be sure that she was neither a propagandist, a Catholic, nor someone selling goods. She was asked "Be ye married?" and when they received a negative answer: "Then why ben't ye married? Ye be old enough." But when they did open up and talk to her with confidence, she learned that they really wanted very much to have proper schools for their children to attend. Another of the things the Pi Phi's did at the beginning was to send a nurse among the mountain people. Her name was Phyllis Higinbotham and she soon found her Columbia and Johns Hopkins university training a bit impractical.

From the early records of the Settlement School may be learned something of the young men it taught, and who went away to the First World War. Here are two typical examples:

> *Dallard Owenby:* training camp, overseas service. This was the first time he had ever been away from home and he writes of wanting to get back to the quiet of the mountains and asks how the hunting and trapping are this year. He left a little wife of 16 who was in our school for a time.
>
> *Daniel King:* called in the summer. Sent abroad almost immediately. Killed in action. Left widow of 15 years.

Gatlinburg had been selected as the location of the Settlement School upon the recommendation of the United States Commissioner of Education. When the project started, Sevier County was furnishing a three-month school for the local children. The sorority teacher took over its thirteen pupils at the end of its short annual term, and proceeded to try to round out the inadequate school year. The results, though slow, were encouraging. By 1936, partly because of the efforts and activities of the sorority, a four-year high school was operating full-term at Gatlinburg. Both the elementary and high schools are located on the grounds of the Settlement School, and are jointly supported by the county, state, and federal governments, and by Pi Beta Phi. In 1951 over five hundred students were enrolled. Every morning during the nine-month academic year, a bus leaves Gatlinburg at 7 A.M. and picks up children at such out-of-the-way places as the Glades, Pigeon Forge, and Elkmont. Graduates of the high school now go to college, and it is interesting to note that most of them choose to return to their mountain homes to help their parents and aid in the advancement of their own communities.

Through the helpful interest of "Aunt" Lizzie Reagan and other members of pioneer families, the venerable art of spinning was revived, and many of the later generations learned this handicraft. The school also encouraged weaving, basket making, and furniture making in the homes, since there was hardly any industry in the region. Weaving is especially popular. The people come to school and receive the raw materials on consignment. When the weaving is completed, the finished products are returned to the school, placed on sale in the Arrowcraft Shop, and the weavers are paid for their work by the hour. According to Miss Ruth Dyer, who has efficiently directed the Settlement School for many years, an average of a hundred local families a year are helped in this way. Chapters of the sorority in all parts of the United States help sell the products, the profits going to the settlement school.

Gatlinburg items are also sold by the Shuttle-Crafters, and by Southern Highlanders, Inc., an organization formed in 1935 to help rural industry and handicrafts, which maintains an elaborate, picturesque shop in Rockefeller Center. Among the other crafts followed by the mountain people are textile decoration, jewelry making, craft design, recreation crafts, dressmaking, tapestry weaving, quilting, and woodworking. Under the guidance of expert teachers, the old art of whittling has been extended to the creation of figures of animals, dolls, and people which would do credit to a sculptor. A heritage of the Smoky Mountains is the weaving of cornshucks into chair bottoms, some of which have lasted for a century. I clearly recall my own grandfather sitting in the shade of a tree after he was over ninety making chairs, smoothing the rounds with a piece of broken glass.

Although time and the opening of the Great Smoky Mountains National Park have brought some modernization to the lives of the people around Gatlinburg, the work of the Pi Beta Phi Settlement School still goes on. The nearest thing to a hospital in the community is the health center operated by the school. Here a registered nurse supervises community nursing, public health instruction, inoculations, and a baby clinic in cooperation with local physicians and government facilities. The resident staff of the Settlement School totals seventeen, who also oversee the operation of a chicken and vegetable farm, a dormitory where rural boys and girls who live too far from the school may stay, and a summer workshop sponsored by the sorority and the University of Tennessee, in which students from all parts of the country obtain academic credits for learning handicrafts.

Education in the Smokies

The census of 1940 showed that there were more children per family in the Smoky Mountain region than in almost any other part of the country. The reasons are not far to seek: lack of birth control, adherence to ancestral customs, and a frequent tendency toward quantity rather than quality. With more children to take care of and less wealth than most places, the Smokies presented problems in health, education, and employment. Especially was there an acute need for more first-rate doctors, nurses, and public health facilities.

In contrast to the large number of children, it was found that the middle-aged people were smaller in number than in the average section. This was because many of the younger generation had migrated elsewhere. The enchantment of distance appealed to their inherent pioneer natures. Friends returning from visits up North and out West told, with the license of the traveler returned, of glamorous attractions beyond the mountains. Some of the young people went North to the big cities, where they could get highly paid union jobs. Others went to the Northwest, where there were fewer people and more land on which to move around. A few went to the northeastern part of the nation, and some journeyed to Texas, and some went on to California to add to that state's oversupply of immigrants. Most of them realized that the distant fields might not be greener, but felt it would be fun to find out anyway.

By the middle of the century, however, the younger people in these mountains and the surrounding areas were at last beginning to realize that their greatest opportunities might be at home. Seeing other places during the war taught many of the servicemen the downs as well as the ups of life elsewhere. Seeing other places also made them realize that much was needed to be done at home.

Books, magazines, newspapers, movies, radio, and even a little television, have done much in recent years to break down the isolation of the upland people. Young ministers have brought religious tolerance, and Jewish synagogues and Catholic churches are not the unfamiliar phenomena they once were. But the school system has remained a drawback, although it is improving. Teachers in the back-country schools have not been too well trained, and a lot of local people would not send their children to them anyway. There has been a compulsory education law for a long time, but it is hard to enforce. As one old farmer said: "There are a lot of folks around here whose children jist won't go to school. You can coax 'em sometimes, and lead 'em if they want to be led, but you can't make 'em do anything."

Dr. Marion Pearsall, a University of Arkansas anthropology professor who made a study of the settlement of Black Gum Gap near Sevierville, Tennessee, found that:

> Formal education is generally regarded as rather frivolous and a waste of time, although the complaint is occasionally heard, "I never went to school much so I can't get any real easy jobs now." Many excuses are made for not sending children to the district school. Some are reasonable — the distance is too great for the small children, there are times when the work of the whole family is needed at home, and the like. Other excuses are: the children are "picked on" at school; parents say they love their children so much they cannot bear to send them to school, but the same parents will leave their children home alone all day.

The foregoing is an extreme example of a ridge community, but it does point up some of the problems confronting educational authorities. In general the schools have improved, and will be even better when the low tax assessments are raised, affording more school funds. There are less of the old one-room schools, and more of the consolidated high schools are new, streamlined, and well staffed. As for institutions of higher learning, the region is fortunate. The University of Tennessee at Knoxville and the University of North Carolina at Chapel Hill are two of the outstanding state universities in the country. In addition, Vanderbilt, Duke, Wake Forest, Maryville College, the University of Chattanooga, and other fine private institutions afford the students of the section excellent opportunities for higher education.

Though library facilities may not be adequate in towns and cities, they are always far ahead of those in the country communities, and the Smoky Mountain region is no exception. Up until the advent of the TVA, which stimulated other government agencies to take action, the books in the back country were few. The stalwarts among them were the Bible, *Pilgrim's Progress,* and Webster's Dictionary until well past the turn of this century; these were about the only literary adornments of many a mountain home, and some did not even have them.

With its vital auxiliary purpose of helping the people as much as their land, TVA started a plan whereby the state and local governments agreed to provide a good variety of books for the most remote homes. This was accomplished by means of mobile library units, a method which has spread over most of the nation. When it came time to leave this work in the hands of the local agencies, some concern was felt about its continuance. There need have been no worry. One woman, for instance, told a meeting of interested citizens that her East Tennessee county had over six thousand people but no railroad, no telephones, no newspapers except the occasional one coming in from outside. The only source of information of this admittedly unusual county, besides a few radios, was "the grapevine and bookmobile." So the residents read four thousand books a month, and the library service affected every family in the county. Needless to say, the service here was retained. It was in other counties too. In the six years from 1940–1946 for example, the people of twelve Smoky Mountain counties read a total of two hundred fifty thousand books, virtually all of these from the mobile library units.

It is hard to feel that illiteracy is extremely prevalent here when one sees back-country people taking to the books like ducks to a pond. The distribution system is simple. Some friendly member of the community uses his living room as a receiving and distributing station for the books, which come by bookmobile from the central library at the county seat. The young and old, busy and unemployed, single and married, all flock to this domestic book collection, welcoming it into their once-isolated lives. No one family could buy all the books which flow through these public channels month after month, but by pooling resources, numerous families for miles around read thousands of books and magazines.

Mainly responsible for the success of the mobile units and remote branch libraries are the government's Bureau of Agricultural Economics and the American Library Association. In the few very isolated communities which they do not yet reach, books are obtained from the state library by mail, the farmers paying only postage. Rural discussion groups have been formed by the National Grange, the American Farm Bureau Federation, and the Farmers' Union, which use the bookmobiles to provide the books and other printed matter under discussion. The average bookmobile is on the road five days a week, making stops at schools, farmhouses, and crossroads stores, even stopping along the roads to lend books to individuals. TVA brought electricity to these regions so that folks could see better to read; the mobile library service is giving them a reason to keep the light turned on.

X

Oak Ridge

On the night of the Bikini atom bomb test, the choir inside the gleaming windows of the Chapel on the Hill in Oak Ridge was singing *Rock of Ages.*

It was a significant coincidence, this song and the momentous event taking place on the distant Pacific atoll. The people of the atom-built town in the shadow of the Smoky Mountains had become solemnly conscious of their part in the destiny of man; and they were expressing this consciousness in the best way they knew, the way of their forefathers.

Oak Ridge began when Lieutenant General Brehon B. Somervell of the War Department Services of Supply met an engineer officer named Leslie Groves in the hall of a Washington government building one day in the hot summer of 1942, and told him he was to have the most important production assignment of the war. Groves was disappointed because he had just been assigned to combat overseas, the first time in his long Regular Army career he had had such an opportunity. But he was soon to be thrust into a harder fight than that of the front lines — the Manhattan Engineer District, official operational name of the atom bomb project. Previously Albert Einstein had sent a memo to President Roosevelt saying he believed an atom bomb could be made, and after deliberation the Chief Executive had decided to risk two billion dollars on it, and sent a penciled note of endorsement to Secretary of War Stimson which read simply *O.K. FDR.*

The project was located at Oak Ridge, whose name not only designated the locality in Tennessee, but because its rustic simplicity would be apt to arouse little curiosity. The name, however, was the only simple thing about it.

When the Army engineers arrived on the ground late in 1942, they found that the name of the place was literally mud — red, oozy mud from clay which was so sticky and hard to dry that it often remained soft and messy underneath even after the surface had become dusty. The engineers took a long look around at the wooded hills and scanty farmland, and wondered how they could bring scientific system out of such natural chaos. But they had no choice. They had strict, secret, urgent orders, orders not only to work but to work very fast.

The Oak Ridge area, eighteen miles from the East Tennessee center of Knoxville, headquarters of the Tennessee Valley Authority, and eight miles from the little town of Clinton, had been selected because of its accessibility to the matchless TVA waterpower; its accessibility to a dependable water source; its remoteness from the coast and therefore relative safety from air attack; its distance from large population and industrial centers; its spaciousness, which could accommodate four different plants all separated from each other by natural ridges to reduce explosion hazards; and its nearness to Knoxville, which had a large, non-critical labor supply.

In the early days of the Manhattan Project, the most numerous inhabitants were quail, rabbits, possums, and skunks. But soon the sleepy villages of Scarboro, Wheat, and Robertsville, which were the focal points of community activity, disappeared, and on their sites stood the huge plants of the Atom City. The farmers then roundabout raised some tobacco, a few hogs, owned a cow apiece, a few chickens, and a generous number of hound dogs for hunting. They were wedded to their land. They even looked a part of their land; and they did not want to give it up. Only a few years before, many of their neighbors had been uprooted by the TVA; most of the Oak Ridge people, being just in the edge of the area, were left alone. Now progress had come to them.

Added to the inhabitants' anger at being disturbed was the thick secrecy which overhung the new project. "The govermint men jist couldn't or wouldn't explain." One oldtimer came to the gates of the Oak Ridge plant and asked the guards what was being built. They answered that they didn't know. The old farmer then said he had heard they were building a new Vatican for the Pope. When told by the guards to go on his way, he cocked his head and asked. "Well, if you don't know what's being built, how do you know it ain't a Vatican?"

But complaining or not, about one thousand families were ordered to vacate their homes by January 1, 1943. The government tried to relocate them where they wanted to be, and paid $45 an acre for their land, which had previously sold for an average price of $40. To some of them, of course, all the money in the Mint would not have been enough to compensate for their loss. One old farmer refused to leave and hid out in the reservation for a whole year before being spotted by the Army.

First came the bulldozers, then the carpenters, plumbers, and electricians. They made their way through the mud to the interior of the vast project to start work on something, they knew not what. Throughout the otherwise empty and ordinary-looking landscape, seventeen miles long and nine miles wide, patrols and sentries suddenly appeared, bristling with guns and signal equipment. Night and day they patrolled the countryside. Signs went up saying *Restricted Area*. At the gates of the project were security police with armored cars.

Recruiting headquarters for workmen was set up in a Knoxville hotel, and word was passed around among workmen in various sections of the country, and among young scientists in universities and large corporations, that the government needed them on a project in Tennessee which would shorten the war. Many workers were obtained from Knoxville and the surrounding sections, some of them, like relatives of mine from in and near the town of Sweetwater, pooling their cars and driving the eighty-mile round trip every day. Some of the uprooted farmers took Oak Ridge jobs. So many interviews were held with each worker and so many forms had to be filled out, that a number of them quit before they got started. Each applicant had to give a minute account of his doings for the past ten years. All the preliminaries were bound up with red tape in its deepest dye, yet the speed with which the whole thing was launched and accomplished was one of the wonders of scientific history.

Making his way along the winding length of the picturesque Clinch River, the new employee reporting to Oak Ridge noticed first the warning signs, then the big fences, the guard towers, and in the background the foundations of the plants to come. The first residential dwellings were three hundred units for the scientists, each of them having a wood-burning fireplace. These were located on an elevated section which later became known as "Snob Hill." Prefabricated houses made of Cemesto, a cross between cement and asbestos board, were brought in and set up, and the working families began to arrive. Some had to live in trailers, thousands of which were parked in designated lots within the outer limits of the area. Efficiency apartments were hastily erected, and crude hutments built by the hundreds. Both white and colored lived in the shack-like hutments, but nevertheless a hue and cry was soon raised in the North that Jim Crowism was being practised. The single men lived in dormitories or barracks. On the hills, demountable houses stood perched on stilts like huge grasshoppers about to take off. Quickly the temporary streets took on such names as Squirrel, Terrier, and Raccoon streets. Helping to offset sectionalism was a road named Abraham Lincoln Drive.

Before long, several smokestacks could be seen rising in the spacious interior area. By this time rumors in the communities around Oak Ridge ran wild. One was that a new rocket fuel was being made; another, that a secret, high-test synthetic gasoline was being refined; another, that the whole project was devoted to the manufacture of silk stockings, Roosevelt campaign buttons, Waac face powder, and dehydrated water for overseas troops. The most elaborate and intriguing rumor was that they were making green paint to spread over the water, so that a submarine attempting to surface would get sea-colored paint over its periscope and would continue to rise until it could be shot down by anti-aircraft guns! Local newspapers asked so frequently for information on the project that finally a congressman announced from Washington that a demolition range for planes and artillery was being built here. Some of the workers became so impatient at not knowing what they were working on that they quit, but the majority remained.

Just who made up the workers of Oak Ridge? First, there were about five hundred soldiers in mufti. In civilian life they had been newspapermen, lawyers, detectives, and the like, all handpicked for this unique assignment. The rest of the 75,000 — to which the town grew in just two years — were mainly mechanics from Detroit, scientists from New York, and farmers from Tennessee. About fifty per cent of the workers came from within two hundred miles of Oak Ridge. The more experienced men were picked to supervise the initial construction and organizational activities, and to act as lecturers in orienting the others. Soon the plants, laboratories, and offices were completed, and soldiers, civilians, and scientists found themselves working together at telephones, typewriters, and gadgets, each doing a single operation that apparently had no relation to the rest of the project. To a meeting of five thousand foremen, Major General Leslie Groves said:

> You'll just have to take my word for it that this is a very important undertaking, the most important of your lives. All I can promise is that if this project succeeds — as I am certain it will — you will never have to be ashamed of the part you played.

Some of the buildings were so huge that few people knew their extent. The gaseous diffusion plant alone consists of seventy buildings, and its four-story main building has wings one and a half miles long. The electromagnetic plant contains one hundred seventy buildings and cost $400,000,000. At the time of the latter's construction, copper was so scarce that a half-billion dollars' worth of silver was borrowed from the Treasury for use as electric conductors — making it just about a billion-dollar building. Inside the plant are magnets two hundred thirty feet long with a pull so strong that it is hard for a human to walk past them because of the pull on the shoenails.

But such facts were unknown to the workers of Oak Ridge in the early days. Each knew only his ordered part. Inside the glass-brick walls, the workers wore white uniforms to prevent dirt and dust, pinned to each a badge designating the unit to which he or she belonged. The thing which distinguished the whole operation was the lack of noise: in hundreds of buildings filled with miles of pipes and countless gadgets and dials watched by girls who recorded only what they were told to, an almost deathly quiet hung over all. Men rode bicycles to get from one connected floor to another. There were Ph.D.'s who apparently did nothing but turn knobs affixed to mysterious thingabobs. At night, the busy buildings resembled long, giant boxes hugging the ground and honeycombed with holes of streaming light.

Running the town of Oak Ridge was not strictly a military operation, although the Army was always active in the supervision and security measures. So many FBI and Army Intelligence personnel lived and worked with the Oak Ridgers on every level that it was impossible to distinguish friend from spy — and sometimes a person was both. The management of the town was actually done by the mammoth Turner Construction Company of New York, which was paid on a fixed fee basis and assumed responsibility for the lighting, paving, water supply, sewage, garbage, and the steam plant. The Army kept its control over police and fire departments, as well as the three hundred-bed hospital, but the private firm maintained the buildings and paid the personnel.

The hospital operation constituted a sort of socialized medicine. Each family head paid four dollars a month for medical services for himself, wife, and all children below nineteen years of age. There were few private calls by the young doctors, most of whom were from the Mayo Clinic, but whenever such a call was necessary, the fee was turned over to the hospital.

Surfacing the three hundred miles of mud-dust streets * was one of the Turner Company's first jobs. Other duties consisted of renting and maintaining the 10,000 houses and apartments, the dormitories with 13,000 rooms, hutments and barracks with 13,000 spaces, 5000 trailers, and a hotel. The houses, which had been built at the rate of one every thirty minutes, rented for as low as $22 a month including TVA electricity and garbage collection. The company also supervised eight elementary schools and a junior high school, having in all 11,000 pupils with 317 teachers.

Religion was a part of Oak Ridge from the start. In this fundamentalist region not many miles from Dayton, a unique institution sprang up. It was just a little chapel on a hill in the atom center, but in it seventeen different religions worshiped. It was called the United Church and had no members; all of its communicants were "associate members," retaining their affiliation with churches back home. (In Oak Ridge today there are six churches and seven Sunday Schools.)

The cultural life was not neglected either. Books arrived

---

* Mud was aptly called the "underlying theme" of the place. Ordinary manners called for removing one's shoes, Oriental-fashion, before entering a house. Because of the tenacity of the stuff, churned up by vehicles, humans, and rain, the dormitories usually had a line of occupants in front of the janitor's sink waiting to wash the viscid Tennessee soil off their shoes. At the formal dances in the recreation halls, girls were known to arrive impeccably dressed in smart evening gowns wearing a mud-caked pair of rubber hip-boots.

almost with the bulldozers, and before the first year was out a fullfledged library was circulating — albeit in a strange manner. It took the form of an Army ambulance, painted by the imaginative librarian to look like a circus wagon with a red, white, and blue fringe. It was called "the surrey with the fringe on top," and moved about the hundreds of miles of streets and roads complete with its books and a puppet show for the children thrown in for good measure. The librarian, Jean Lowrie, found herself trying to answer questions from a cosmopolitan audience such as she had never seen before. Chief among the queries were those concerned with local geography, history, and the recreational facilities. Miss Lowrie's comment on her work is significant:

> You simply never knew from one day to the next what unexpected thing would develop. But it was fun. Working with children who lived perhaps in a house, perhaps in a trailer; children who came from every state in the Union and who had lived in almost every other state or perhaps even abroad; teachers from all over bringing new thoughts, creating new classes — such things have more than compensated for the uncertainties of living and working under pioneer conditions.

For diversion, community services were created in the form of theaters, bowling alleys, nurseries, riding academies, a roller skating rink, an amusement park, dancing classes, a poolroom, an art school, and a junior band. There were all kinds of athletics; twenty-five thousand persons played tennis at various times. With half the workers being native Tennesseans, the square dance flourished, and scarcely a week went by that did not include one or two hoedowns in the recreation halls.

People learned to joke about their strange new life. There

were known to be two ways of getting into town: one was to stand on a street corner until a bus came along; the other, to stand in an open field until they built a town around you. A wartime sign which originated in Oak Ridge and later was seen at defense plants all over the country showed a picture of a turtle and the caption: *Behold the turtle; he makes progress only when his neck is out.*

Everything was not rosy at Oak Ridge. Four men moved off the job to one who stayed. Even though this unique city was the only one in the country with no unemployed, no extreme wealth or poverty (as it has remained), the wartime working conditions were monotonous. Due to the extreme secrecy, the workers could not see the results of their labors and consequently had nothing tangible in which they could take pride. The carload after carload of material which rolled into Oak Ridge seemed only to disappear; "much went in but little came out." A Philadelphia doctor, Bernard M. Blum, investigated and reported that poor housing conditions endangered the health of workers more than did the making of the atom bomb. According to his investigation, meningitis was five times more prevalent in Oak Ridge than elsewhere, with Negroes being stricken more often than whites and men being three times more liable to the disease than women. In a report to the American Public Health Association, Dr. Blum ascribed this condition to poor housing, exposure, and fatigue, saying that environment rather than the economy of the individual was the determining factor. The situation was soon remedied, however.

Perhaps the most striking characteristic of the unique community was the effect of security measures upon the residents. One worker said that even those who talked in their sleep learned to keep their mouths shut so that their wives could not learn what was going on. Remarked he: "There was a time when, after coming home from work, I couldn't talk to my wife at all. I had an idea what the project was making but I couldn't tell her. We'd sit around the dinner table and the strain was terrible. A man could bust. Then we started quarreling. So we decided to have a baby."

It is true that there was an unusually high birthrate in Oak Ridge during wartime. The number of births was ten times the number of deaths. Perhaps some explanation of this was the inducement held out by the rule that those who had an additional child could move from an A-house to a superior B-house and so on to an F-house, depending on the increase of children. Those who married moved from a barrack to an A-house. The youthfulness of the population was also a factor, most of the workmen being under thirty years of age and the scientists, as a rule, under forty.

On August 6, 1945, Oak Ridge reached its climax. The atom bomb was dropped on Hiroshima.

What Oak Ridge had been doing was dramatically expressed in the announcement of President Truman:

> Sixteen hours ago an American airplane dropped one bomb on Hiroshima. That bomb had more power than twenty thousand tons of TNT. It is an atomic bomb. A harnessing of the basic power of the universe.

At first the people of Oak Ridge, with few exceptions, were just as astonished as anyone else. They did not know until hours later that they had had more to do with the momentous event than other war workers. But by the middle of the afternoon the realization began to dawn on them that they had fashioned a new age — the atomic age. Informed now that much of the secrecy veil had been lifted, they felt relieved. Then as the full significance of the event sank in, they were overjoyed. These people who had been pent-up and confused for so long went around crazily shouting new words which they had not been allowed to use before:

"We're making uranium here. Uranium–235!"

Newspapers from Knoxville sold out so fast that they soon were bringing a dollar apiece. The Oak Ridge *Journal,* the local weekly, ran a headline: *Oak Ridge Attacks Japan.* Old signs which read You Can Lick Japan were taken down and in their places were substituted You Hold the Key to World Peace.

The Oak Ridge people were reverently conscious of what they had made. They gathered in their chapel and prayed. Two months after Hiroshima, the Oak Ridge *Journal* carried the results of a survey made among the workers. They were asked: "What form of control do you favor for the atom bomb?" Of those interviewed, four-fifths expressed themselves in favor of some form of international control, the rest stating they felt the United States should keep the bomb as a potent means of insuring world peace. Oak Ridge High School students were told by atomic chemist Charles Coryell that unless the atom bomb was controlled, one out of every three of them would probably die of the effects of atomic energy. Alarmed, the students formed a youth council dedicated to control of the new and terrible energy.

The end of the war witnessed a large voluntary exodus of people from Oak Ridge. The excitement, the temporary, frantic activity was over. Since the government could not give the workers who remained in atomic production any definite assurance that the project would be permanent, many of them made their way back home or elsewhere to jobs with unquestioned permanence. Within a matter of months, the population of 75,000 dropped to less than half. The Roane-Anderson Company, the Turner subsidiary which ran the community, trimmed its operating force from 10,000 to 4000. Concessions were let, but it was difficult at first to attract chain stores; however they are today at Oak Ridge in force. The Government furnishes the buildings but not the fixtures. Rent is paid on the basis of receipts; for example, a store with a monthly gross of $10,000 pays the Government a rental of $1000, and no business is allowed to make more than a ten-per-cent profit. To business interests, Oak Ridge is like a government bond, giving a safe but low return on invested money.

With the coming of peace, the labor situation in Oak Ridge also changed. During the war emergency, Under-Secretary of War Robert Patterson got AFL President William Green and CIO President Philip Murray to agree not to try to unionize the project's workers. After V–J Day both these labor organizations rushed to organize Oak Ridge, now less restricted. Still, the Army checked the labor organizers carefully and forbade them to canvass from door to door. In 1946 three NRLB elections were held in Oak Ridge amid considerable mudslinging on the part of the competitors. Epithets of "Communist" and "racketeer" were exchanged freely. One union, the night before an election, issued a card offering a hundred-dollar reward to anyone who could prove that the other was untainted by Communism. At the U–235 plant, the CIO won. The AFL was victorious at the electro-magnetic plant. Workers at the third plant voted not to have a union. A strike vote was taken in 1947, but a stoppage was avoided by a ten-cent increase in pay plus other concessions.

On January 1, 1947, the Manhattan Project was officially transferred to the newly formed Atomic Energy Commission.

However, it was not until April 9th that the commission itself was fully functioning because of the delay in the Senate confirmation of David Lilienthal, the chairman. The long and bitter proceedings which preceded his approval by Congress raised many doubts about the atom project, and brought to the minds of Oak Ridgers the impression that atomic science got too mixed up in partisan politics. During the hearings, Lilienthal gave his famous vest-pocket definition of American democracy, which has been admired and considerably quoted since by people of all political leanings.

> I believe that all government and all private institutions must be designed to promote, protect and defend the integrity and the dignity of the individual. . . . Any form of government, therefore, and any other institution which make means rather than ends, which exalt the state or any other institution above the importance of men, which place arbitrary power over men as a fundamental tenet of government are contrary to that conception, and therefore I am deeply opposed to them. . . . Democracy is an affirmative belief rather than a belief against something, and I deeply believe in the capacity of democracy to surmount any trials that may be ahead.

In the transition from wartime project to peacetime atomic center, a more normal operation has been the chief objective. The three plants now include one for separating Uranium–235 from U–238 by the gaseous diffusion process, operated by the Carbide and Carbon Chemical Corporation; another for separating U–235 from U–238 by the electromagnetic process, operated by the Tennessee Eastman Corporation, a subsidiary of Eastman Kodak; and the Clinton Laboratories, a research and development center operated by the Monsanto Chemical Company. The main streets of the city have been curbed and guttered and are hardly recognizable as onetime muddy trails. Trim white houses stand neatly along paved thoroughfares, children playing on the grassy lawns while their mothers gossip across the fences or in the neighborhood stores like those of any other American city. Most of the adults of the community belong to at least two of the one hundred twenty-nine civic clubs which sprang up at Oak Ridge after the war. They are even safety-conscious; at the town's main intersection is a huge billboard on which is recorded the number of days since the last local traffic death. After each fatality — indeed rare in this city — a big red light on the sign burns for seven days; the rest of the time, a green one burns. Oak Ridge also has an enterprising daily newspaper, the *Oak Ridger*, replacing the earlier mimeographed weekly. A local radio station also serves the community.

Early on the morning of March 19, 1949, Oak Ridge became an "open city." Before a large gathering of residents and visitors, a puff of smoke from a small "atomic explosion," set off by an electrical instrument in the street, mushroomed up into the sky and thus signaled the lifting of restrictions on the community. Inside the smaller area where the plants are located, however, the restrictions remain, and bid fair to do so until mankind's mutual trust exceeds any degree it has ever reached thus far.

Oak Ridge is still, at this writing, under the management of the Roane-Anderson Company and under government supervision, although plans have been made to convert it to a normal city. The bus companies, hospitals, and other civic activities are subsidiaries of the Atomic Energy Commission, which reports directly to Congress and which is still the real boss of the project as well as of the community life. The city manager of Oak Ridge is selected by the commission; town councilmen represent the people, and consult with the manager in their behalf.

To the observer, it is obvious that life in Oak Ridge is as level as Hiroshima after the bomb fell. The great scientists and the workers live side by side. There is no slum or swanky neighborhood, no "across the tracks." People from the North, East, and West mingle happily with those of the South. This situation is the natural result of a national enterprise drawing people from everywhere to work at government salaries (the average individual income in Oak Ridge was $4139 in 1951). Everyone knows about how much his neighbor is making, which in itself is a leveling influence. Everyone who lives in Oak Ridge must work; there are no leisurely plutocrats, no jobless paupers. All the residences are owned by the government, and there are no mansions and no hovels. The conveniences and the recreation facilities are about the same.

Oak Ridge has several shopping centers, one high school, one junior high school, and nine elementary schools, all of conspicuously fine design. Two branches of Knoxville banks are located in the city, three movie houses, and two drive-in theaters. A spacious auditorium at the high school was opened in 1951, and here the Civic Music Association brings eminent artists to perform. The Oak Ridge Symphony Orchestra, composed of local citizens, practises and gives concerts in the auditorium, which is also used for public dances.

Doubtless because of the high average caliber of the population, little gambling is reported in Oak Ridge. Its police department has picked up a slot machine now and then, and a numbers racket on a minor scale was once discovered operating in a section of the city having the appropriate name of Gamble Valley. There is little prostitution, though officials, when asked privately, admitted that "there are bound to be some loose girls around." Seldom are robberies reported, and murders even less frequently.

Though at Oak Ridge the citizens live lives comparatively free of crime, bad health, slums, and delinquency, the substance on which they work is very definitely a matter of life and death — the result of what General Groves called "a generation of scientific achievement compressed into three years." He told me that when the Oak Ridge project began, atomic energy development was at the stage where the automobile was at the beginning of this century. Three years later, he said, it had progressed as far as has automotive science since 1900.

At the Oak Ridge National Laboratory, one hundred thousand mice are studied to determine radiation effects. One of the greatest hopes of the researchers is to find out whether some of the approximately fifty radioactive materials that can be produced in an atomic pile will serve as a means of preventing cancer.

Another significant phase of the atomic energy program, especially as far as the South is concerned, is the Oak Ridge Institute of Nuclear Studies. This has been formed by twenty-six Southern universities, and its aim is to stimulate cooperation between the federal government and the universities in atomic research, through the unique facilities of Oak Ridge. Life here has been found to be more intimate, quiet, and otherwise suitable for scholarly concentration and research than in the big cities. Many prominent Southern scientists have already taken advantage of this opportunity to work in the restricted laboratories of the Oak Ridge National Laboratory and to establish research programs which are then continued at their individual universities. The institute has a ten-million-dollar expansion program underway, and it also makes grants of millions of dollars to Southern universities for research — with no government strings attached. The University of Tennessee conducts agricultural research on a three thousand-acre tract near Oak Ridge through arrangement with the Atomic Energy Commission. Here experiments are made on both animals and crops, using radioactive materials to study such things as the effects of atomic explosions on cows, and the use of radio-isotopes in plant fertilization.

An exhibit entitled *Man and the Atom,* which explains atomic energy by vivid and simple scale models, pictures, and maps, has been set up as a nucleus of the American Museum of Atomic Energy at Oak Ridge. The exhibit is a center of attraction for the hundreds of thousands of visitors who come to see the Smoky Mountains and Oak Ridge. In 1950 and 1951, part of the exhibit was put on wheels and shown at state fairs. A highlight was a stunt in which two hundred and fifty thousand volts of static electricity were conducted into the body of a girl from the audience, making her hair stand on end but not harming her at all.

When in 1942 the government surveyors first appeared at Oak Ridge, the people of the region naturally had no idea that here would arise a city which would be "an epicenter of a physical and moral force that has altered the destiny of mankind and his world." Today they have accepted it as part of their life. Dr. Russell Poor, chairman of the University Relations Division of the Oak Ridge Institute of Nuclear Studies, was one of a number of people attending the funeral of an obscure farmer. No minister was present, so the undertaker asked: "Would someone care to say a few words about the departed?" There was a deep silence. Again the under-

taker repeated his request, and again no reply. For the third
time he asked: "Would not *some one* like to say a few words
about the departed?" whereupon Dr. Poor arose and said:
"Well, if no one wants to say anything about the departed,
I'd like to say a few words about Oak Ridge."

XI

Smoky Mountain Holiday

Of all the Southern highlands from Kentucky and Virginia through Tennessee and North Carolina down to Georgia, the most vivid manifestation is the Great Smoky Mountains National Park. It is the government's answer to a long-standing desire of Southern people to perpetuate these mountains in their natural state. The movement to establish the park started over a half-century ago, but it was not until May 22, 1926, that the park was authorized by Congress and the first land set aside. Since then more land has been acquired by the states of Tennessee and North Carolina, aided by federal funds and a contribution from John D. Rockefeller, Jr., in memory of his mother, Laura Spelman Rockefeller. Today the park contains 440,000 acres, located just about evenly in North Carolina and Tennessee. It is supervised and cared for by the National Park Service.

The mountains within the park are classed by geologists among the oldest on earth. For about one-third of their length they have an average altitude of over five thousand feet. Several of the peaks reach a height of more than six thousand feet; Clingman's Dome, towering 6642 feet, is the highest, and is exceeded east of the Rockies only by Mount Mitchell in North Carolina. Along these summits hovers at nearly all times the dreamy blue haze from which comes their name of Smoky Mountains. Only hard rains or dense clouds disturb it, and not for long. There is a fascinating attraction about these mountains for the visitor, whether he is looking at them for the first time or seeing them again. They are not the most rugged of highlands, but they have a lasting allure that is not forgotten. Their foothills are soft and inviting, their most remote peaks bare, lonesome, and mysterious.

In the Smokies were found the first hardwood forests of America. Today this botanist's garden holds two hundred thousand acres of sycamore, elm, gum, willow, persimmon, chinquapin, beech, birch, basswood, magnolia, cucumber, butternut, sourwood, box elder, ash, maple, buckeye, poplar, hemlock, oak, hickory, pitch pine, locust, and dogwood. For many years the chestnut tree dotted this region with its green leaves and prickly burrs, but the nationwide blight dealt a sad blow to those who still recall the deliciousness of the small chestnuts so gingerly extracted from the sharp burrs.

The park has more than twelve hundred species of flowering shrubs and plants. Here grow twenty kinds of orchids, fifty kinds of lilies, twenty-two kinds of violets, and five kinds of magnolias. In the spring the blooms follow a logical rotation: the mountain laurel opens in May and June; the flame azalea, which the eighteenth-century botanist, William Bartram, called "the most gay and brilliant flowering shrub yet known," blooms in June; and July finds the rhododendron out in full flower. Earlier the mountain woodlands are carpeted with smaller flowering plants. In July the giant mountain lilies appear at the higher altitudes. Fall brings the striking spectacle of leaves changing from green to brilliant autumn hues that set the mountains aflame.

For too long a time, heartless hunters scoured the mountains, often killing females bearing young as well as the males of native animals. With the coming of the national park, officials have cut this vicious practice to a minimum. Some of the less law-abiding residents would seine the creeks for fish, even dynamiting them at times, and thus keeping down the normal increase of the fine bass, trout, and perch. But now there is an abundance of game in the forests, especially deer and bear. There are two hundred species of birds and more than fifty species of fur-bearing animals. Fishing is seasonally permitted on six hundred miles of mountain streams. Snakes abound in the deepest coves of the mountains, but the two varieties found most, rattlesnakes and copperheads, rarely bite anyone unless molested. There are no mosquitoes up in the Smokies, but the common housefly is all too common. The careless hiker will pick up plenty of chiggers, perhaps some fleas and wood ticks. In the streams leeches may attach themselves to exposed flesh, but can be easily removed. (Leeches are still used by some of the mountain people to treat black eyes and varicose veins.)

The climate is variable. The region has one of the highest annual rainfalls in the United States, around 60 inches and more in the mountains (by comparison, New York City has 44 inches, the Scottish Highlands 130). There are an average of 155 clear days each year, about 100 partly cloudy, and 100 cloudy. Few real droughts or unusually rainy spells occur; the Smoky Mountains serve as a buffer against the eastward flow of the upper air currents, and thus help to distribute their moisture in an even and pleasant way. Blizzard weather has been experienced here during some exceptional winters, but ordinarily the temperatures from the middle of December to the first part of April do not go below fifteen to twenty degrees above zero at the coldest, and most of this period is much warmer. A winter day in the uplands may have rain, sleet, snow, freeze, and thaw, all in the space of twenty-four hours. The summer days are warm, their nights usually cool.

Here and there may be seen old Indian trails and former Indian campsites. Various artifacts, such as arrowheads and eating utensils, have been found, indicating that the Cherokees, who inhabited and claimed the region from about 1623 until their removal westward, penetrated into the most remote parts of the Smokies. Less than four thousand of the red men now remain, living quietly on the Qualla Reservation in the edge of the park at Cherokee, North Carolina. Other reminders of yesterday in the Park take the form of old cabins with porthole windows and dog-trot openings between the rooms; and now and then visitors will run across an old moss-covered water mill to which mountain boys still come on muleback with a turn of corn to be ground into meal. And according to reports, there is still found in this federal government park an occasional moonshiner, plying his clandestine activity in some sequestered cove until discovered and flushed out.

Some of the earlier residents who sold their land to the government for use as part of the park did so with the understanding that they could live here the rest of their lives. Most of the five thousand families, however, exchanged their hillside farms for a house and lot in nearby towns or villages. A few moved far away. Those who remain, and who are removed from their isolation into public view, have been the butt of numerous and absurd jokes, which doubtless inspired the famous sign found in front of one of the mountain homes:

NOTIS

Tresspassers will be persecuted to the full extent of 2 Mungrel Dogs which never was over sochiable to strangers & 1 Double Bbl shot gun which aint loaded with sofa pillows. Dern if I aint gettin tired of this hellraisin on my place

Parts of the topography are unique. On the high summits of some of the peaks are "bald spots," bare except for grass. Below these odd-looking empty areas, the rest of the mountain down to its foot is covered with trees. The cattle, sheep, and hogs of the early settlers found good grazing there. Several families used the same pasture areas, cooperating in herding and salting their flocks. Livestock raising became one of their most profitable pursuits. There has come down from these early upland shepherds a logical wisecrack which may still be heard to this day: "That feller lives so fur back in the hills, he has to look up his chimney to see if his cows are comin' home."

Place names — Dirty John Creek, Burnt Shirt Mountain, Bloody Branch, Black Rock, Naked Place, Shake Rag Branch, the towns of Vest and Suit near Murphy, N. C., Glory Ridge, Four Killer, Arbutus Ridge, Tumbling Creek, Mammy and Daddy Creeks, the village of Loafers Glory, Easy Ridge, Mad Sheep Mountain, Long Hungry Ridge, Chunky Gap Mountain, Buzzard Roost, Dog Slaughter Creek, Miry Ridge, Broken Leg, Desolation Branch, Raw Dough, Piney, New Hope, Happy Hollow, Fighting Creek, Ball Play, Greasy Branch, Little Bullet, and Gouge Eye.

Ten years after its opening, the first President of the

United States to visit the Great Smoky Mountains National Park, Franklin D. Roosevelt, drove over the skyline drive to Clingman's Dome. A number of Tennessee and North Carolina congressmen accompanied him from Knoxville over the Smokies to Asheville and on to Charlotte, where he delivered a speech. When the trip began it was a bright, sunny day, but by the time the twenty-eight-car caravan reached Newfound Gap, misty clouds were hovering over the peaks. Suddenly down came a drenching rain so typical of the region, and wet many of the presidential entourage. It was noontime, so FDR sat calmly under the canvas top of his touring car and ate his lunch of hot dogs. Never to be outdone on traveling, Mrs. Roosevelt visited the park the next spring. Instead of finding balmy weather, she encountered cold and snow. But she was delighted with her visit. In her column *My Day* she called the Smokies "enchanting." Her lunch was more elaborate than that of her husband, consisting of country ham, green beans cooked with pork side-meat, cauliflower, hot biscuits, cornbread, mountain honey, cottage cheese, coconut cream pie, and coffee — a typical meal now served to tourists. The Roosevelts were to visit this park on later occasions, and their fondness for it did much to establish it as a national tourist attraction.

This is one of the few national parks open the year around. One enters it through the main gateways at Gatlinburg, Tennessee, or Bryson City, North Carolina. There is no entrance fee. Maps and logs of scenic loop trips, and information about accommodations and the like, are available at the park headquarters in Gatlinburg. There is no charge for parking and permits for camping may be secured (camping is limited to three days). Tourist camps, homes, and hotels are available in all the towns near the park. Many people stay in Knoxville or Asheville and motor from there, while others prefer the smaller places or roughing it in the open.

Cats are not permitted in the park, dogs must be held on a leash. The speed limit for cars is thirty-five miles per hour. No fires may be built along the roadside except at designated campsites, and no trash may be scattered. Rules prohibit one from throwing stones at the birds or animals. Trees, shrubs, or plants must not be disturbed. Visitors are not allowed to feed, handle, tease, or otherwise bother the numerous bears, which can easily become dangerous pests if at all encouraged.* At some of the main tourist stops the visitor may hire a private open-topped automobile with a chauffeur, and ride through the surrounding mountains for an enjoyable view. Sightseeing buses leave Knoxville, Gatlinburg, and Asheville on conducted tours; one of the most popular of these is the one hundred-mile scenic round trip which begins and ends in Knoxville, going by way of Maryville or by Sevierville, two of East Tennessee's historic towns.

Gatlinburg

The opening of the Great Smoky Mountains National Park, the advent of the Tennessee Valley Authority and

---

* Driving from Gatlinburg to Cherokee one late afternoon, we came upon a number of automobiles stopped beside the road, and saw that the object of attraction was a big black bear standing at the edge of the adjoining woods. Following the example of the others, we stopped, and I grabbed a camera and approached rather close to take pictures of the innocent-looking bruin. My wife, small son, and daughter were standing a few feet away, when suddenly the huge animal wheeled and without warning took a mighty swipe with his front paw at our daughter. My wife barely managed to get her out of his reach in time; they could feel the bear's hot breath on them as he lunged dangerously close, almost brushing their clothing. It happened within a few seconds and practically paralyzed the rest of us with fear. Needless to say, it was a lasting lesson about friendly bears.

the lakes and parks which resulted, the increased boating, hunting, and fishing, the good and convenient roads, all have made the public aware of this magnificent vacation land in North Carolina and Tennessee. A foremost example of the constantly enlarging tourist trade is Gatlinburg. Situated on the edge of the park about forty miles east of Knoxville, Gatlinburg today hums with tourist activity. But as late as 1910 the people who lived around the village were still subsisting on barter, which isolation made necessary. The community was still trying to recover from the effects of the Civil War. There were few roads, and those which existed were bad ones with no bridges; consequently, travel to and from the quiet little mountain village was extremely light and mainly on foot. The beauteous mountain scenery which never fails to impress, the bracing air and coolness even in hot summer, were known to few. Life was much the same as in 1776. Each family had a muzzle-loading rifle, a tiny garden plot scratched out of the hillside, and a fishing pole — with which three items they provided their food and clothing. They buried their own dead, placing the bodies in wooden boxes covered with black calico; and instead of tombstones, pictures of the departed in glass containers were set on top of the graves. Modesty prevailed; as recently as 1925, Gatlinburg boys refused to play basketball in shorts unless they wore their "overhalls" underneath.

In 1950 two million visitors came to the Great Smoky Mountains National Park — a record for all national parks in the United States — and their effect upon Gatlinburg may be judged by statistics. In 1940 the population of the town was 1700, while in 1950 it was 2500, an increase between national censuses of about forty per cent. In 1940, the total bank assets of Sevier County, in which the town is located, were $1,878,335, while ten years later they were approximately $7,000,000. In 1940, main street property in Gatlinburg sold for $50 an acre; today this same land is appraised at $8000 an acre. The land adjoining the resort has also skyrocketed in value; one nearby farm which sold for $15,000 in 1935 recently was sought for $50,000, and the offer was turned down.

With the exception of a small knitting mill and a smaller canning factory, Gatlinburg has only one principal business — tourists. In 1940 the town had facilities to accommodate about 1000 persons. Today the six modern hotels, two lodges, and fifty tourist courts have a total capacity (usually filled) of 3000 persons a day. The total tourist investment is about $7,500,000. The Gatlinburg Tourist Bureau has estimated that each visitor spends an average of seven dollars a day for food, lodging, and recreation — which is comparatively little, but which runs into many millions annually for the resort. A stroll along the main street is a cross between visting in the open country and meandering at a carnival. Hotels, restaurants, and curio shops beckon the visitor with beguiling signs, while fellow tourists stuffed with food and laden with souvenirs gently jostle each other on the wide, smooth sidewalks. Over here is a shop dealing in handicrafts of the Smokies, the Indian theme predominating, while opposite is a tiny tavern from which drifts the plaintive strains of "good old mountain music." Above and beyond, the majestic backdrop of the Great Smoky Mountains themselves, standing impressive and clear against the horizon, forms an unforgettable image of nature at her very best.

Prior to 1940, when the park was formally dedicated, there was still a good deal of the earthy speech of the Smokies spoken in Gatlinburg; but since the influx it is hard to find anyone who speaks the quaint language of yesterday. From the older generation and from some of the remaining settlers who still cling to their cabins in the coves around Gatlinburg, one can yet hear it; but though recordings have been made of many of the old songs as sung by the settlers, there still remains the job of saving the speech of the Smokies for posterity by means of adequate recordings of conversation. Mrs. Edna Lynn Simms, one of the veteran residents of Gatlinburg, has collected many examples of the speech of the early settlers, which she keeps in a card file. Once a well-known clubwoman and writer herself, she has become wary of some of the feature writers for magazines who come to see her, find out all they can, then, as she says, "misrepresent the mountain country and its people and don't give credit where credit is due." Mrs. Simms now spends her time overseeing a picturesque establishment called the Mountaineer Museum, which is as full of authentic relics as her head is filled with the lore of the Smokies. In it are over two thousand items, from a snuffbox to a spinning wheel, which she has gathered from the mountain people during her quarter of a century here. Visitors who come to see the pieces hear lectures on their historic origin.

Highlight of the museum is an eighty-year-old cabin with all its original furnishings. Mrs. Simms tells a story about the owner of the cabin when he lived in it high up in the mountains years ago. It seems that a visitor from Kentucky gave him a few plants of burley tobacco, which the mountaineer characteristically accepted with reluctance, but finally planted in his garden patch. When she saw him a few months later, Mrs. Simms asked him if the burley was any good for smoking. He replied it was so good it had set all his women folks to smoking. And how was it as "eatin' terbaccer"? he was asked.

"Misris Simms, I'm a-tellin' ye the truth," he replied. "That's the finest eatin' terbaccer I have ever saw. Why hit's got about one thousand spits to the chaw!"

Four families own Gatlinburg, or almost all of it — the Ogles, Whaleys, Maples, and Huffs. They lived here when there was little to own except ordinary mountain land, so there is something nice about the new wealth staying in patient old hands. The Ogles own the big store and the other three families own a hotel apiece. The most prominent leader among the local people was the late A. J. Huff, who founded the Mountain View Hotel, the resort's first inn. Always eager to keep Gatlinburg in local hands, he is said once to have loaned money to another owner who was having a hard time keeping his hostelry. In these hotels local people make up the staffs, and they take an interest and pride in doing a good job that is refreshing after one has seen so much of the other type of service in various parts of the country. One unfortunate tendency is that many of the souvenirs and other items for sale here and in the stores are cheap, factory-made stuff instead of the genuine local handmade articles, although there is still a fair amount of the latter on display.

A notable event which has been held in Gatlinburg for several years, and which reached such proportions in 1951 that it was transferred to Asheville, is the annual Craftsman's Fair of the Southern Highlands, at which representatives of the handicrafts of the lower Appalachians demonstrate their skills, and where plans are made for the coordinated progress of this important activity. One of the newest crafts in the mountains is the weaving of nylon string into handbags, something which started out as just another tourist-catching item. It has become one of the leading income industries in the Smokies. The weaving is strictly a hand operation, with whole families pitching in to dye the nylon string, twist it into a yarn, weave the fabric, and stitch it into handbags. Some families have bought electric sewing machines, run by TVA power, to help speed up their production. Wholesalers order forty to fifty thousand of the colorful bags a month. They tell the master weavers what they want, these in turn farm out the orders to the different families — who still insist on selling their handiwork for cash only.

To know Gatlinburg is to know Wiley Oakley, wanderer and guide, called the "Roamin' Man of the Mountains." Seated on his front porch while the cool air from the nearby Little Pigeon River wafted through, Wiley, a medium-sized man with a face that bespeaks his Indian ancestry, told in a pleasant, nasal voice of his fifty-five years in these parts. He started wandering about the mountains as a child, looking for his mother, who had died. He never could believe but that "she had jist gone off into the woods fer a spell." Although he never found her, he did find the peace that comes with mountain solitude, and now reflects it in his philosophy of wanting to help others.

Unlike many, Wiley wants to remain just a mountain man, and he accordingly dresses in the simple overalls and boots of another era. He knows the Smokies as perhaps no other man does, and takes people to any part of them — for a fee, of course. Once he walked, now he rides with the visitors in their nice cars until they get as far back in the mountains as automobiles will go. Typical of his kind, he revels in understatement regarding his exploits. But he owns his home in Gatlinburg, has a big rustic gift shop which furnishes free mountain music, and, with his guiding activities, evidently does all right. Wiley writes ungrammatical pamphlets, as well as a column for the local newspaper, the Gatlinburg *Press,* which is run by a pair of enterprising Yankees, Mr. and Mrs. William C. Postlewaite.

"Hit takes courage to remain a mountaineer," Wiley says, "but hit pays."

Wiley Oakley likes people to be as happy as he is. In addition to working for money, he does many spontaneous kind deeds for his friends and for his many acquaintances who visit the Smokies. He gets letters of thanks from "little people from the country and big'uns from New York and other cities" who have had him as their companion and guide. He believes in enjoying everything about him every day. Once, after he had been on the radio, he was taken to New York and offered a high-paying contract. He grinned, turned it down, and returned to his beloved Smokies to resume his quiet life. Said he: "I wasn't gonna sell my birthright for any mess of potash."

Near the neighboring community of Montvale lives a man called the "Thoreau of the Smokies." His name is Bert Garner and he is no dyed-in-the-wool-hat hillbilly either, having spent years of his life in Philadelphia working for the *Saturday Evening Post* as — of all things — the official in charge of returning rejected manuscripts to writers. Past middle age, Bert now lives all alone in a cabin squarely in the middle of a thirty-acre patch of woods. In his old house he has no electricity, telephone, plumbing, or any of the other modern inconveniences. He doesn't want them. He prefers to live close to nature. Bert goes barefoot part of the time, and when he wants to, wears his shirttail out, because it's more comfortable and nobody much sees him anyway. He

reed
 liv-
 the
swer
rica.
onds
club-
from
ne —
tion.
 and
bear,
, the
tains
Rus-

ad to
 shift
 them
 over
 into
 from
eased
ed at
uper-
mals,
lland
of the
tled"
Ten-
Fish

ouring water into a big tin can perforated
oisting it up to the limb of a tree, and
th. His house is filled with books, and he
re money for books than food — most of
ses himself, grinding his own meal. When
 Bert and heard how he "saved Cousin
g herb remedies. His father, a herb doc-
d the life" of my own mother, after the
l given her up.

thin and graying, lives here alone, like his
 He does it simply because he loves the
solitude. He did not always live alone;
he didn't like the woods, so she picked up
 Washington, D.C. Oh yes, Bert has an-
 keeps snakes in the house. Pet snakes,
ous ones. They kill rats better than cats,
nore, he likes 'em.

Wild "Rooshian" Boar

there have been in certain parts of the
ferocious wild boars known to many local
" wild hogs. These dangerous animals
bjects of exciting annual hunts, attracting
ber of avid hunters from all parts of the
ild boar is no ordinary sport. It is one of
t dangerous, and in more romantic days,
y the sound of horns and the prancing of
s used spears, bows, and arrows. Some of
en removed from the hunts in Tennessee
a, but none of the danger.

How these hogs got into the Smokies is generally
upon. In 1912 a group of wealthy English businessm
ing in New York had the idea that a game preserve
wilds of the Great Smoky Mountains would be the
to their dreams of a happy hunting ground in A
Headed by George Gordon Moore, the group sold
among themselves and used the money to build a larg
house and other buildings near Hooper's Bald, not fa
Robbinsville, North Carolina, close to the Tennessee
one of the wildest and most primitive forests in the
A six hundred-acre tract was enclosed by a high fen
within this enclosure were loosed some cinnamor
pheasant, elk, buffalo, deer, and about fifteen wild bc
last-named having been brought from the Harz Mo
of northern Germany and from the Ural Mountains
sia, habitats similar to the Smokies.

When the First World War came, the Englishmen
return to their own country, and so left the animals
for themselves. In 1920 an attempt was made to hun
within the enclosure, but they became excited, jumpe
or broke down the fence at several spots, and escape
the surrounding woods. The only ones that survive
the expensive experiment are the boar, which have in
in number with the years until today the herd is estim
six hundred. Forest fires, natural causes, and lack of
vision contributed to the disappearance of the other a
but the hogs found outside the fence a type of wo
suited to them, with acorns, berries, and roots. Some
boar remain in North Carolina, but most of them "s
in what is now the Tellico Game Management Area
nessee, under the supervision of the State Game an
Commission in Nashville.

The wild "Rooshian" boar is king of his domain, and a description may explain why. This huge, wild-looking hog weighs up to four hundred pounds. He has shaggy, silvery hair and is built like a small buffalo, his lean, muscular body rising from short, strong rear legs, over which flops a mule-like tail, to large, powerful shoulders and a vicious head. From his long, pointed jaws there curve upward razor-keen tusks usually six to eight inches long, with which he can inflict mortal wounds on dogs or men. Sometimes dogs which get too close are disemboweled in a moment by these lethal tusks, which, with his sharp hoofs, are his offensive weapons. For defense he has a layer of thick cartilage over his maned shoulders which will stop a hound's jaw or an ordinary rifle bullet. Dense fur and bristles cover most of the rest of his skin. The "Rooshian" boar can take on and lick three dogs at a time. Unpredictable, he will turn on hunters and run them up trees. It may seem fantastic, but he can run faster than the average deer, and has been known to keep up a running fight with dogs at full speed over rough terrain for as long as twelve hours.

The boar hunts are conducted regularly and systematically under the supervision of the Tennessee State Game and Fish Commission and the United States Forest Service. Fifteen three-day bear and boar hunts are allowed each year, with not less than eight or more than twenty hunters in a party. The season runs from the middle of October to November. There is a limit of one bear per party, but the boars are so dangerous and numerous that they can be killed without limit. Individual still-hunts for bear, boar, and deer under the same rules are permitted in November and December. Experienced guides with dogs are available at Tellico Plains in East Tennessee.

When the ban against boar hunting was first lifted, the few hunters who ventured in had several of their dogs slashed beyond further use, and some of the less-careful were themselves wounded. Since then they have become more cautious, though the hunts are still full of hazard. Any hunter out to bring home this unique kind of bacon must also keep in mind that, in addition to roots and berries, the wild boar also likes to eat rattlesnakes, so these reptiles are apt to be encountered. Plenty of stamina is required for pursuing the hogs in this area, which is part of the million-acre Cherokee National Forest and one of the few remaining isolated forests in the United States. The undergrowth at times is almost impenetrable, and one never knows when a boar may pop out of a laurel thicket. The hunter must always be prepared with either a rifle (at least 30-caliber) or a bow and arrow, the latter weapon often proving surprisingly effective against the tough hide of the boar. He must wear bramble-resisting clothes and be able to travel full speed on foot and over steep hills for hours at a time. Courageous dogs with lots of endurance are required, such as those raised by the Plott family of Waynesville, North Carolina.

The dogs bay the boar when they get its scent. Then they go after their prey, the hunters following, and both giving the animal a wide berth until he is tired out and bayed. The older hunters usually place themselves in stands until the boar passes by — if he does. Should a hunter get in the way of a boar, it will rush him, and if he misses his shot he will have to take to his heels, for a wounded boar is compared by those who have hunted him to a Malay tiger or to a lion.

Three of the most enthusiastic of the local boar hunters are Mr. Milton Thompson, Dr. R. S. Hines, and Colonel James F. Corn of Cleveland, Tennessee, who each year lead a group of visitors into the nearby hills for the sport. Dr. Hines spends all his spare time in the Smokies. Colonel Corn tells of the time when he was to escort General Jonathan Wainwright on the hunt. The evening before there was a dinner for the hero of Bataan in a Cleveland hotel and the colonel was asked to say grace. Somehow General Wainwright got the idea that Corn was a chaplain, and next day, while both were standing for a long time in one of the cold, uncomfortable stands waiting for a wild boar to pass, the general would not take any of the moonshine proffered him, believing himself to be in the presence of a gentleman of the cloth. When finally, after many dreary hours had passed, he accidentally learned that Colonel Corn was a reserve officer and a prominent local attorney, Wainwright, with a big snort, changed his mind.

XII

Smoky Politics Today

THE Smokies have always been a place of picturesque politics. From the days of Sevier and Jackson through the turbulent times of Polk and Johnson and on up into the current days, the course of true Smoky Mountain Country politics has never run smooth.* One reason is simple: upper East Tennessee is normally Republican, a conservative island in the usually unruffled sea of Southern Democracy.

This part of the nation likes its politics dramatic and color-

---

* The story is told of a candidate for political office who was electioneering in this region soon after the turn of the century, and who recalled his military service with Generals Scott and Custer. "Fellow citizens," he said to an assembled group, "I have fought against the Indians. I have often had no bed but the battlefield and no canopy but the sky. I have marched over the frozen ground until every step has been marked with blood." All gazed at him impressed, except a dried-up-looking voter who came up to the front.

"Did you say ye'd fit fer the Union?" he asked.

"Yes," replied the candidate.

"And agin the Indians?"

"Yes, many a time."

"And that you had slept on the ground with only the sky fer a kiver?"

"Certainly."

"And that yore feet bled in marching over the frozen ground?"

"That they did," cried the exultant candidate.

"Then I'll be danged effen ye hain't done enough fer your country," said the voter. "Go home and rest. I'll vote for the other feller!"

ful, like the War of the Roses. Sometimes it even goes over-board, such as just after the Second World War, when a disgruntled group of returned soldiers at Athens, Tennessee, decided to revolt against the corrupt political machine entrenched in the county government. These ex-GI's, fresh from the battlefields of Europe and the Pacific, decided, because ordinary measures had failed, to use their newly learned military methods to remedy the situation. Following a "fixed" election, they armed themselves with formidable weapons from the local armory and besieged the local authorities in the jailhouse, riddling it with bullets from an ambuscade across the street. When the celebrated revolt was over (by some miracle no one was killed), the officials had left the county, and in their stead was a new kind of layman's government led by the servicemen. How well it has adhered to the principles of good government advocated by its leaders is hard to say; but at least McMinn County had a new and violent opportunity to clean its political skirts.

There have been other election shootings at Athens when death resulted, as there have been in the neighboring county seats of Madisonville and Benton. In 1951 an official of Polk County, of which Benton is the seat, was ambushed and the county government thrown into an uproar. Undesirable national publicity followed, especially when armed members of the two opposing political factions moved down from the nearby Smoky Mountains, and when the vital activities of the local government were paralyzed by the deadlocked votes of the members of the county court. In a campaign reminiscent of the War of the Roses, two brothers, Jeff and Clint Wilson of Polk County, ran against each other for the vacancy created by the murdered man, the former winning as a nonpartisan candidate against a faction of Democrats. Actually it is not accurate to compare this minor race with that idyllic and peaceful campaign of the Taylor brothers in 1886, for by mid-century Polk County had so bloodied up its local politics that Governor Gordon Browning considered recommending to the legislature that it be broken up and parceled out among other counties.

A happier example of East Tennessee politics was twenty-three-year-old Miss Mary Shadow of Rhea County, who while in college wrote a paper on politics and, when she handed it in, remarked that she did not like the political situation in her own county. "Then why don't you run for office and clear up the mess?" she was asked. She did just that in 1950, defeating the veteran Walter White, of Dayton trial fame, for the state legislature, thus becoming the youngest woman legislator in the nation, and the only woman in the Tennessee legislature. Her campaign consisted mainly of direct appeals to the people, and cost her a total of $270. Although attractive, Miss Shadow would not use her sex to attract votes; in fact, she took her mother along on her campaign so that men would not bother her. While in the legislature in Nashville she had fourteen offers of marriage, finally accepting one from Dr. David L. Hill, an atomic physics professor at Vanderbilt University.

Extensions of the local Saturday courthouse lawn sessions are the all-day barbecues and dinners-on-the-ground. In spite of radio and television, the local folks still like personal appearances by a political speaker, especially when he has a hillbilly band and is a good spellbinder himself. This too has been carried to extremes, as in the case of the host-candidate who arose after a succulent repast and read to the large crowd a speech which had been written for him. He got along all right until the end, when in his eloquent onrush to the climax he capped the finale with the words: "March forward with me into the dawn of a new day! Pause for applause."

An uncle of mine tells of a Smoky Mountain candidate he heard on one occasion. Two other speakers preceded him to the stand, both giving long harangues about the problem of taxes. The audience was obviously exhausted. When the third candidate arose, he shifted his eating tobacco from one side of his mouth to the other and said simply:

"Folks, there's jist two things about these here taxes that I want to say: if they're too high, we'll lower 'em; if they're too low, we'll hist 'em."

He sat down. He was elected.

The current Smoky Mountain system of county government with its elected squires dependent on political support has been sharply attacked as ingrown and inefficient. Virtually everything depends upon who wins the election; all the "ins" go out and the "outs" come in, the latter probably knowing nothing about the operation of government and the former leaving just when they were learning. Remedies for this situation are being studied despite the howls of local politicians who would be hurt by changes in the system.

Kefauver, Browning, and Crump

Conspicuous among campaigns that have held the state and national limelight in recent years was the race of Gordon Browning and Estes Kefauver in 1948 against the powerfully entrenched Ed Crump machine of Memphis. Kefauver, with whom I grew up, was reared at Madisonville in the shadow of the Smokies, and his campaign was colorful and unorthodox.

In the first place, Kefauver, then congressman from the Third District, announced his candidacy for the Senate almost a year before the election, though such early announcement was considered political heresy by most politicians. But he wanted to become better known, to acquaint more people with his unusual name (which is pronounced "*Kee*-fah-fer"; one opposition speaker constantly referred to him as "Cow Fever"). So he went all over the state, into each of its ninety-five counties, shaking hands with thousands of people in all walks of life — and they liked it. Another "mistake" he made was failing to consult Boss Crump, who for twenty years had ruled the state, naming governors, senators, and congressmen as well as controlling the legislature. Crump held sway by virtue of the fact that his overwhelming control of the sixty thousand votes of the city of Memphis enabled him to swing any election in this sparsely voting Southern state. He was called the "last of the big city bosses," and it is said that Huey Long learned some of his prowess from him.

Crump was a master of invective, too, and the early-bird senatorial candidate was not long in getting a sample of it. Referring to Kefauver's liberal leanings, the white-maned Memphis dictator stated that he "would as soon vote for Marcantonio as vote for Kefauver." This was supposed to knock the young candidate right out of the ring — and it almost did. It took him a long time to live down the unjustified comparison. At first he tried not to antagonize Crump, but soon the Boss ran full-page newspaper advertisements all over the state referring to Kefauver as a "pet coon who puts its foot in your bureau drawer and when you catch him, looks the other way, pretending that he was doing nothing wrong."

The candidate replied: "I may be a pet coon but I'm not Mr. Crump's pet coon." The crowds laughed — and this time at the Boss, something unprecedented in his long reign. A smart young public relations man suggested to Kefauver that he don a coonskin cap and capitalize on the accusation, so at his next speaking engagement Kefauver did, and it brought down the house. From then on this colorful furpiece became the symbol of the campaign, and is acknowledged to have played a major psychological part in the outcome of the race. Whenever Kefauver failed to put on the cap at the start of a speech, his audiences would begin to chant. "Put it on, put it on, put it on!" until he would have to stop talking and do so. He called this a "sort of strip-tease in reverse."

During his trips around the state, in which he literally shook twenty-five thousand hands, Kefauver systematically recorded and acknowledged the friendly contacts he made. He or his campaign manager or his wife, who accompanied him, made notes and afterward sent personalized letters of different types to those called upon. There was one slipup in this procedure, however. In canvassing Carthage, the home of Representative Albert Gore, an intimate friend of Kefauver's with whom he had served in Congress for years, Gore's name somehow got into the wrong envelope, and he received a letter which began: "Dear Mr. Gore: It was certainly nice to make your acquaintance, and I shall look forward to knowing you better as time goes on . . ."

Into Memphis went the Kefauver entourage, violating another Tennessee political adage that no opposing primary candidate dared go into this lion's den. Apparently the young aspirant had not learned the orthodox rules very well, for he not only went into Memphis but spoke there boldly defying Crump and all his henchmen — causing some of Kefauver's followers to fear he would meet with personal violence, as others had done in the past. A Committee for Kefauver was even formed in Memphis, composed of prominent businessmen who wanted a change from bossism.

Former Governor Gordon Browning, another enemy of Crump's who had been seared with his billingsgate, announced he would run again for governor. The Boss had paid him the compliment of saying he was the type "who would milk his neighbor's cow through a crack in the fence." But the candidacy of Browning, who was very popular, was a great boon to Kefauver, and from then on the gubernatorial and senatorial candidates fought shoulder to shoulder against the dictator in Memphis.

A Memphis newspaper editor, Edward J. Meeman, came out courageously in favor of Kefauver. Crump challenged him to be judged by a local committee on his stand, or leave town. Kefauver took up the cudgels, wired Crump that he would answer the challenge, but stated that if he won he did not want anyone to have to leave Memphis. "That is Joe Stalin's way, not mine," the candidate added. No more was heard of the matter.

Kefauver asked his two opponents, both "Crump-puppets," to meet him in public debate. They consistently refused. So he tried to catch up with them, arriving at their speaking places just as they were finishing, rushing up on the platform with a ringing challenge for them to stay and have it out with him. They never did. He labeled them both "hit-and-run speakers."

The Negroes of the state came out in unprecedented force and worked and voted for Kefauver. They liked the candidate because of his long fight against the poll tax, which prevented many of them from voting, and because of his stand against the filibuster. They also liked his advocacy of the use of federal funds to equalize educational opportunities for whites and Negroes. The labor unions favored him, admiring his firm stand for the TVA and against the Taft-Hartley Act, although he pointed out that he had also voted for the Hobbs Anti-Racketeering Act to make unions subject to certain anti-trust laws. In respect to voting for any law, Kefauver explained: "I call them as I see them."

Predominant in the victory forces for Kefauver were the women of the state, a strong voice in Tennessee politics ever since they had pressured their men in the legislature to pass the final ratification of the Nineteenth Amendment. The distaff side liked Estes Kefauver. Not only was he handsome and gallant in true Southern style, but he had a pretty, devoted wife and three fine children — making a well-rounded American family, the kind voters like to see a candidate have. Mrs. Thomas Ragland, wife of a Chattanooga manufacturer and an official of the League of Women Voters, became his state chairman, and under her vigorous leadership the women got busy. When it came to carrying the fight to the Memphis stronghold of the Boss, the female element was the vanguard of the attack, thus making things even harder for old Ed Crump, who prided himself on being a Southern gentleman and quite chivalrous with the ladies.

Not so in his attitude toward Browning and Kefauver, however. In another of his newspaper advertisements, Crump paid compliment to Browning in the following manner:

I have said it before and I repeat it now, that in the art galleries of Paris there are 27 pictures of Judas Iscariot — none look alike but all resemble Gordon Browning; that neither his head, heart nor hand can be trusted; that of the 206 bones in his body, there isn't one that is genuine;

that his heart has beaten over two billion times without a single sincere beat.

On primary election day, July 5, 1948, the results were decisive. People who had always been afraid to vote against the Crump machine showed no such fear this time. As one citizen said: "I pulled my hat down over my eyes and voted for Kefauver. I'm going to own my soul from here on."

The Kefauver-Browning ticket won by a decisive margin, giving Crump his first defeat in twenty years.

Now the two victors faced two East Tennessee Republican candidates in the general election in November, usually an unimportant anticlimax for Democratic voters. Not this time. Even as the Crump defeat echoed through the nation, Kefauver announced he faced a hard fight. It was the Dewey-Warren year, a conceded Republican presidential victory; and added to this was that fact that the former Republican national chairman, wealthy B. Carroll Reece, was running for the Senate after several terms in the House, with Roy Acuff, the fabulously-popular hillbilly singer, as his running mate for governor. This duet of opposites decided to inject a new note into the Republican strategy in Tennessee — a musical note. They hired Acuff's string band and started out to cover the state with mountain music interspersed with a little politics. They drew big crowds, who came mainly to hear the music; but for a time it looked as if the state might have its first elected Republican senator since the Civil War, and the capitol a hillbilly governor in the tradition of Pappy O'Daniel of Texas and Jimmie Davis of Louisiana.

Their campaign was another hark-back to the War of the Roses when Robert and Alf Taylor traveled the state and fiddled and sang from the same platform. Reece hired a high-powered Washington press agent, Carlisle Bargeron, to publicize the show. Bargeron wrote back to his journalistic friends in the capital that he could not figure out what all the commotion among the mountaineers meant. "I can only tell you at this stage," he said, "that at one little place an old-timer chewing snuff said: 'I ain't voted in twelve years. I got plumb disgusted. But I'm agonna vote this time — for that fiddler and the feller who's runnin' with him!'"

Even so, Kefauver and Browning won this one too.

Progress Not Perfect

Seeking a location for a new branch plant, a prominent Northern manufacturer inspected fifty-five communities in eight Southern states. After more than a year of investigation into characteristics such as suitability of plant site, potential operating costs, and the like, a Smoky Mountain community was ranked first. Yet the plant was finally built elsewhere in the nation.

The reasons given by the manufacturer for his rejection of the local site are interesting, and typify the needs still remaining in a region which has so many natural advantages. The manufacturer was offered low taxes. He didn't like this, even though his county taxes would have been only $440 a year, whereas in some of the other places considered they would have been as high as $75,000. The company officials stated that they expected their firm to carry a fair tax load. Otherwise, they did "not see how the community could furnish proper schools, recreation, sewers and city services for their employees." Recreational facilities were obviously lacking; there was no good park or municipal golf course, and the only visible means of diversion was a moving picture theater and a poolroom. The educational facilities were also inadequate, the company officials concluded, stating that they wanted the best such for their employees' children. Community pride, too, was considered lacking. A large number of homes needed painting and many business houses were old and ugly. There were colored slums about which no one seemed concerned. There was no local airport, and company executives needed to fly from their distant headquarters back and forth to the new plant. Especially noted was the fact that there was not a first-class restaurant in the town; although some good small eating places were found. Fuel costs were higher than at many of the other places considered. The local labor supply, both male and female, was regarded as inconsistent and inadequate (this was disputed by civic officials).

This community may not be an average example, but it demonstrates the fact that an attractive place to live is not enough; facilities must be well rounded and demonstrable to outsiders, if new wealth and development are to be attracted. For a long time, local people did not want to bring in strangers, particularly Yankees; but recently, in the more progressive parts of this mountain country, new industry has been courted and won in spite of a few old families who wanted to keep things "just as is" until they died. One civic official, when asked what his shabby town needed, replied: "A few good funerals."

It is good to report, therefore, that the other side of the picture is not only brighter but bigger. Tennessee and North Carolina have in recent years been called the fastest-progressing part of the nation. A few examples of industrial development in and near the Smoky Mountain Country show that private capital is at work here as well as government resources. The spectacular parts of the latter may sometimes cause one to lose sight of the increasing momentum of the former.

Soon after the First World War the Eastman Kodak Company learned that the woods around Johnson City and Kingsport, Tennessee, were a fine source of the wood alcohol used in the making of Kodak film. The company purchased land and timber rights, and built a modern sawmill as well as a twenty-mile logging railroad. Since alcohol making required only the limbs and tops of the trees, the company was also in the lumber business before it knew it. Then, in the early 'thirties, it was found that home movies were growing so much in popularity that better fire protection for them was needed. Non-inflammable film was the answer. The perfect substance for making such film was cellulose acetate, which is cotton treated with certain chemicals. Kingsport, near a good cotton supply, was selected for a huge plant, and the resulting Eastman operations at Kingsport have become the largest in the country. A printing plant, the Kingsport Press, produces millions of books a year for publishers in New York and other cities. Johnson City, not to be outdone, has shipped out in the past ten years enough hardwood flooring to build a four-foot boardwalk around the world four times (according to Carl Jones, prominent local newspaper publisher).

Knoxville is the headquarters of the Tennessee Valley Authority. It is also the key city for tourists entering the Smoky Mountains from the west. On the east, in North Carolina, Asheville, a wholesale, financial, and transportation center, as well as a superb resort, is the main hub for visitors entering the mountains from that direction.

Bristol, on the Tennessee-Virginia state line, is a bustling business town and railroad junction which has added considerable new industry. About forty years ago, two brothers named Stokely raised some tomatoes on their farm near Newport, Tennessee, and got their mother to can them. They sold some, people liked them, so they began canning other vegetables. Today the Stokely Company is one of the largest canners in the nation, and one of its plants is still near the site of the original kitchen at Newport.

A few years ago a Hindu student asked the U.S. Department of Agriculture where he could best study community organization among farmers. They sent him down to the Boone's Creek community near Jonesboro, Tennessee, where a community club was in operation. How it works is described by the experience of Mr. and Mrs. Lee Carter, who moved from Johnson City to a farm in this community. At first they hardly ever saw any neighbors, much less got acquainted with them. Then the Community Club was formed, the people all got together, held contests for better homes, had social gatherings, raised money for a Parent-Teachers' Association, and beautified the schools and churches. Commented Mrs. Lee: "We are much happier. There is no word in Webster's Dictionary that can describe the power such clubs have to bring families closer together."

Looking ahead, it becomes obvious that the further development of this region, as of other parts of the South, must be accomplished mainly by Southerners themselves. Dr. Robert D. Calkins of the General Education Board in New York City expressed this thought in a speech:

> The Southerner needs more confidence in his capacity to do things in the South — big things that are now considered impossible. . . . No one but the Southern people themselves can or will make Southerners prosperous. Outsiders may help. They can be induced to contribute capital and

know-how and other forms of assistance, but fundamentally what the South reaps it must sow, and what it does not sow itself, it will not reap.

Customer Number 1,000,000

Chester Williams feels that he was a lucky man. He happened to be the one-millionth customer to get TVA electric power. The press release about the event explained that Chester was actually "a consumer, not a customer," because TVA can sell only to municipalities and cooperatives, which in turn sell directly to all individuals, including Chester and his apple-cheeked wife.

There was quite a ceremony at the Williams' Oakview farm, the TVA information officials being no novices at handling opportunities for good publicity. The program included a barbecue — sure to bring a crowd — and a lot of greetings and congratulations from neighbors and friends, county agents, representatives of cooperatives as well as from county, state, and national government officials. In all there were about two hundred people milling around, shaking hands and anticipating the festive feed. Mrs. Williams was presented with a new washing machine. Chester was slapped on the back as if he had done something special to deserve this celebration. On the back porch of his home were arrayed in dramatic disorder old stoves, coal-oil lamps, a washtub complete with rubbing board, and ancient black kettles, all of which bespoke more vividly than official words the transformation that had taken place on the one hundred-acre Williams homestead. One of the TVA directors, James P. Pope, made a speech. He said, among other things:

In 1933 there were only 15,000 electrified farms in the valley. Today there are about 300,000. When TVA began, only a little more than three per cent of the region's farmers had electric service. Now two-thirds of the farms have electricity. The remaining one-third are being electrified at the rate of six to seven thousand a month.

Fifty-year-old Chester Williams listened with great interest. Now and then he glanced at the electric lights in his living room, the new radio, the gleaming refrigerator in the kitchen near the electric stove, the home freezer, the clothes washer, and the electric water pump outside. "These new contraptions are sure goin' to relieve my wife and me of a lot of work," he said. As for Mrs. Williams, she was more outspoken. "I guess we're an average farm family," she remarked. "We've been on this land for twenty-five years, but until the TVA and REA came along, there was little chance of getting even electric lights. I think TVA is the most wonderful organization that ever operated anywhere."

Looking Forward

If John Sevier could return to his beloved Smokies he would be amazed. He would find the mountains as first he saw them — rugged, beautiful, eternal. He would find the wild game inhabiting them, since its replenishment, nearly what it was in early times. And the mysterious smoky haze that dwells perpetually on the high bosoms of the wooded pinnacles he would find still unidentified, as it was two centuries ago. What Sevier would find changed is the people.

The founders of the new civilization wrested from this wilderness were dreamers, as pioneers always are. Their eyes, straining ever westward, were made glad when they first looked down these mountains to the fertile valleys below. Pausing in the cool shade of the summits, they looked forward along the trail and dreamed a good dream — a dream of the sunlit spring, the tranquil summer, the harvest time of fall, the snows and ordeals of winter, and the rich, warm spring coming around again among these peaceful mountains. Could they know of the progress made in our time, they would feel that their dream had come true.

The pioneers would be pleased that the upland people have for so long preserved the ways of life handed down to them. These ways are good and simple, and therefore they have lasted. True, there is still a long way to go. There is always a long way to go toward the end desired. The training and education of the people have not prepared them, at least until recently, to take a proper part in many of the activities of the world outside these mountains. Their boys and girls have gone away after higher education, but the local folks are still inclined to interpret the world from their traditional frontier viewpoint. They still love the old, comfortable freedom, and hold that respect for family unity and religion are far more important than education and ambition to get ahead in this world. But on the whole, the descendants of those who opened up the mountain country have wrought well.

A list of their achievements would greatly overshadow the roll of shortcomings. They had to wring peace from the savage Indians and savage beasts. They massed behind Andy Jackson at Horseshoe Bend and New Orleans, and made him famous; then they came home to serve him well when he was in the White House. They furnished another President to the nation in James K. Polk, helped him win the Mexican War, and acquired the illustrious name of the Volunteer State. With painful reluctance they were drawn into the Civil War between the States, and brother literally struggled against brother in the saddest and most devastating chapter of the conflict. And in the Reconstruction days which followed, their Andrew Johnson came close to sacrificing himself upon the altar of impeachment in championing the rights of the Southern people. The fury of war gave way to the hatred and suspicion of an uneasy peace, but out of the strife-torn atmosphere a new order did gradually emerge, to become a sturdy part of a nation that was now stronger than ever. Those who felt that things as they were could be improved without violence, set themselves to making a better economic and social life. Even with the growth of industry and the centralization of business, there was still want in the midst of plenty. Outside this region, a great progressive movement swept the country, an organized effort to make better the lot of the common people, but it never got over these mountains.

The turn of the century saw a static society in this mountain country, too isolated to be affected by outside influences, too content to change itself. But change it did. Railroads wormed themselves into the Smokies and brought the sawmill to the trees. Good roads were built, bringing the remote districts closer to progressing civilization. A period of plenty, and then depression fell upon the land. The CCC boys appeared, and TVA; and a dark cloud from Oak Ridge mushroomed over Hiroshima and brought the Second World War to an end. Now it was that everyone realized the full significance of what the government was doing in this picturesque part of the country. For the first time, war plans which had included the long-range development of TVA were revealed to show that the planners, even in the 1930's, had foreseen some such emergency need as that brought on by this war. That the activities would culminate in Oak Ridge, however, hardly anyone could have dreamed.

What is the Smoky Mountain Country today? Electric light in the mountains and valleys, sparkling from the peaks and gleaming from the coves and meadows. Verdant, balanced crops on once-eroded slopes that now hold the rainfall in the roots of planted saplings. Cattle living, not starving, on a thousand hills. People camping in neat parks along miles of water's edge, and boating on man-made lakes. Fish cavorting just beneath the surface, so many of them that in spite of all the anglers ninety per cent die of old age. Factories that once would have located up North beginning to abound in this natural setting where supplies, labor, and good markets are plentiful — seven new plants every day open their doors for business. New building construction showing the highest rate of increase of any part of the nation. Rural telephones slowly increasing. Net incomes higher from cotton, peaches, milk, corn, beef, cattle, sheep and wool, forest products, fruits and vegetables, poultry and livestock. The paper and pulp industry showing signs of rivaling the long-established textile business. A phenomenally increased tourist trade. Within the homes, electrical devices reflecting the innovation they have wrought in the happy faces of their owners. But it is in the *minds* of these people that the greatest transformation has taken place. They have a new sense of belonging to this land.

The people of the Smoky Mountain Country, who for so long adhered to things of the past, can well look to the future. Their confidence is based on the evident symbols of progress and change: a better economy; a higher standard of living; a new realization of the power of the people. Those who have lived on this land for so long, view it now with a new respect. They are just beginning to realize what great things it holds for them, and not only for them but for people everywhere. This is the most significant social laboratory in the nation. Parents are proud and thankful that their sons and daughters, instead of following the venerable custom of going away to make their fortunes, now eagerly return to the rich opportunities at home. Throughout the storied land, an awakening has come.

Index

32621

F
443
G7
C3

CALLAHAN, NORTH
  SMOKY MOUNTAIN COUNTRY.

DATE DUE

10/1/52 ← Pocket Inside

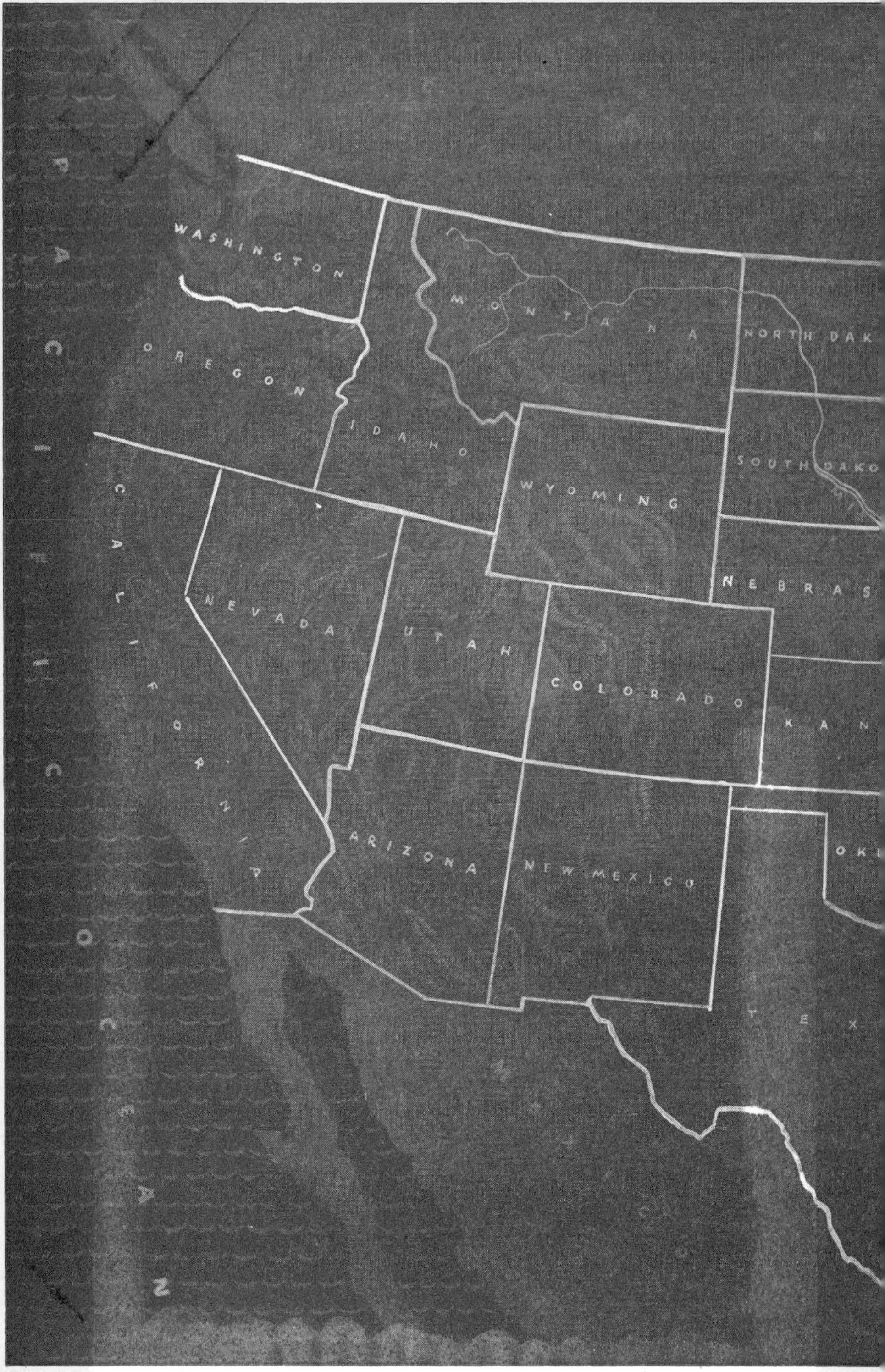